Ormond McGill

For Magicians Only

THE ENCYCLOPEDIA OF GENUINE STAGE HYPNOTISM

By Ormond McGill

Illustrations by MAC

Martino Publishing
Mansfield Centre, CT
2010

Martino Publishing
P.O. Box 373,
Mansfield Centre, CT 06250 USA

www.martinopublishing.com

ISBN 1-57898-871-3

Cover design by T. Matarazzo

Printed in the United States of America On 100% Acid-Free Paper

For Magicians Only

THE ENCYCLOPEDIA
OF GENUINE STAGE
HYPNOTISM

By Ormond McGill

Illustrations by MAC

Published by
Abbott's Magic Novelty Co.
Colon, Michigan

CONTENTS

Preface

In the public's mind Magic and Hypnotism have always been very closely associated, and a Magician is generally conceded to be, also, a Hypnotist. For that reason, few kindred arts can fit as naturally into the Magician's repertoire as exhibitions of Hypnotism. Unfortunately, however, very few Magicians have ever mastered this skillful practice and have thus missed a most valuable adjunct to their programs.

But now comes a ready solution; for here in this book is a complete revealment of the **inner secrets of Stage Hypnotism** presented in the very logical manner by first showing what Hypnotism is, and what it can do through actual instruction in how to hypnotize, and then proceeding directly on, into the modus operandi of Stage Hypnotism itself. The little subleties, insights, and techniques that come only from careful research and practical presentation, are also given, making this book one of the most valuable of its kind ever offered Magicians.

Magic has long had a need for a text book on GENUINE STAGE HYPNOTISM, and Ormond Mc-Gill has wonderfully filled that need.

Percy Abbott.

Introduction

There was a time in theatrical history when exhibitions of genuine Stage Hypnotism were among the top popular entertainments. Then came the fake hypnotists, who, using stooges combined with stunts bordering very closely to the vulgar, soon reduced what had been an extremely refined, interesting, and thought-provoking program into little more than a burlesque farce—and the hypnotic show became a "thing of the past."

Time has gone on, however, and in that period, scientific research in the subject has progressed, until, today, Hypnotism is once again rapidly coming into its own. Hardly a day goes by that one cannot find some newspaper or magazine article commenting upon some aspect of the subject. Psychology and psychiatry have progressed, and hypnosis has gone right along with them. Hypnotism is in the public eye; Hypnotism combines both the intrigue of the scientific and the glamour of the mysteries—**a new era for the hypnotic entertainer is here; an era to which the Magician falls the natural heir.**

It is doubtful if any form of entertainment could be more basically appealing than the hypnotic exhibition. There is something so warmly human, and something so utterly fascinating about watching one's friends react to hypnotic suggestions that it makes Hypnotism stand unique in the entertainment field. Normally staid audiences have been literally convulsed with laughter in watching the antics of good hypnotic subjects upon the stage, and then a few minutes later, that same audience has leaned forward in their seats staring in wonder at the phenomena unfolding before their eyes. The alert Magician, ever in search of the sensational to add to his program, can unquestionably find in Hypnotism one of the greatest talk-producing features he could possibly acquire.

Thus this book is written for the modern magician; taking you from the very beginnings of learning to hypnotize to the culmination of staging the complete hypnotic show.

May mastery and success be yours.

OBTAINING THE FIRST SUBJECT

The practical way for the Magician to commence the study of Hypnotism is first of all to learn how to hypnotize. It isn't wisdom, though, to plunge directly into the production of the trance, however, as many persons have a natural dread of entertaining an unconscious state which may result in your experiencing difficulty in obtaining a suitable subject with whom to practice . . . **and the obtaining of your first subject is your very first consideration.**

To this end then it is best to apply a little diplomacy, and gradually introduce the proposal of hypnotizing to your volunteer. Further, at this initial stage, it is doubtful that you would have much success in completely hypnotizing the subject as many persons can be effectively influenced by lighter hypnotic phenomena who can not be readily placed into the somnambulistic state; and for our beginning in learning the art of hypnotizing, it is most desirable to achieve results right from the very start—**for to be a successful Hypnotist, nothing is more important than to have confidence in one's ability to hypnotize; and nothing builds confidence like success.** Not only is this true in your case as the Hypnotist, but likewise in that of your subject, as his confidence in your ability to hypnotize him increases steadily as he finds himself responding, step by step, to your experiments; as you thus lead him diplomatically towards deep hypnosis.

So, try this approach: Find some congenial person who you feel would make a suitable subject to practice on; turn the conversation towards psychology and comment on the interesting fact that many persons find it most difficult to really relax, and then propose this little test in relaxation.

Now, there is nothing especially new or exciting about this first experiment; but it possesses the advantage of arousing interest without antagonism, and gives you an opening wedge favorable to proposing more advanced experiments. Also it is possible to work it on one person alone or on a group.

Explain that the ability to achieve success in obtaining complete bodily rest, comes in direct proportion to the ability to relax; and that many persons think they know how to relax when in reality they are tense the majority of the time.

To illustrate the point, have the person, or persons, as the case may be, raise his left arm up at a right angle out in front of his chest, then extend the forefinger of his right hand and place it directly under the palm of his left hand. In such a position the extended finger is ready to support the entire weight of the left hand and arm (See Fig. 1).

FIG. 1

Now tell him to completely relax his left hand and arm—the extended finger of the right hand being the sole support to that arm. He is thus in a situation that requires the relaxing of the left arm while at the same time concentrating on holding it up with the extended finger of the right hand. (You have here a situation requiring both concentration and relaxation at the same time—a condition very similar to that required for the induction of hypnosis.) Next, being sure that his left hand and arm are completely relaxed; at the count of "Three," you request him to quickly draw the finger of the right hand rapidly down to his lap.

You then slowly count, "One, two, three" . . . and what happens? If the subject has followed your instructions and performed the experiment successfully, the moment he withdraws the support from under his left hand, that arm naturally drops limply to his lap. Such is the obvious result if the arm is really relaxed (See Fig. 2). But, as frequently proves the case, in

FIG. 2

many instances the left arm of some persons will remain still suspended in the air after the finger support is withdrawn. When this happens, naturally it indicates that these individuals have not relaxed as you requested (See Fig. 3).

FIG. 3

So explaining again that often a person thinks he is relaxed when in reality he is still decidedly tense —as illustrated by the arm that did not fall—you repeat the experiment, requesting that he be sure this time that his left hand and arm is really completely relaxed, the forefinger of the right hand again being the sole support to that left hand and arm. Once more, at the count of "Three," you request him to rapidly withdraw his extended right forefinger from under the left hand. And this time, he is almost sure to have succeeded in obtaining the desired state of relaxation.

Having completed your first experiment in relaxation successfully, explain to your potential subject that another interesting curiosity of the mind to consider is the fact that when an idea is held strongly enough in it, it tends to realize itself in unconscious moments. William James called this affect "Ideo-Motor Action." You are now ready to try some further experiments.

SOME PRELIMINARY TESTS

Ask your subject to stand erect with his feet together. Explain to him that in this experiment you will illustrate this point in unconscious movements, and that he will feel the affects in a inclination to fall directly over backwards. Explain that you will be standing behind him; thus he need have no concern about falling as you will catch him; that he is to let himself go and actually fall right on over backwards as he feels the desire. Further advise that he is not to try to fall; neither is he to resist falling. He is merely to be relaxed and passive, and is to think of the ideas of falling over backward which you will give him . . . and that as he does so he will feel a very definite and distinct drawing sensation pulling him right over backward.

Now, as he stands erect with his feet together, his head up, and hands relaxed at his side, ask him to close his eyes and relax his muscles. You can ascertain that he is doing as you direct by putting your hand on his shoulder and pulling him back slightly. If your subject sways back easily he is doing as you direct; then step behind him.

Standing behind your subject, place the side of your right forefinger lightly at the base of his brain (at the nape of the neck), and tilt his head backward just a bit so it rests lightly upon this finger (See Fig. 4).

FIG. 4

Now, in a low, monotonous voice suggest, "In a few seconds you will begin to feel an impulse to fall ... a sensation of falling right over backward. You are beginning to feel it now. You are beginning to fall— to fall—to fall right over backward into my arms. When I draw my hand from you, you will slowly fall back, backward, right over backward."

In giving suggestions always speak in a calm, positive tone without haste and without raising your voice. Keep your voice kind, but at the same time let there be no doubt about your authority and the fact that you expect your suggestions to be obeyed.

As you present these suggestions of falling over backward ... slowly, very slowly, draw your left hand along the side of his head in a gentle stroking motion. Draw it directly back from your subject's temple until it clears the rear of his head. At the same time gradually lighten the pressure of your right forefinger so that he can scarcely feel it touching the nape of his neck, and say, "Now you feel the influence getting stronger . . . it is drawing you back. You are falling backward—falling backward." Simultaneously with the presentation of these suggestions, continue repeating the sliding back of your left fingers in the slow stroking action along the side of his head. Gradually, as your subject commences to sway, stroke your left hand clear and free of his head, and in this motion also remove your right hand very slowly from the nape of his neck, so that your hands are clear behind him and ready to catch him as he falls, as you continue to suggest, "You are falling backward—you are falling backward." (See Fig. 5).

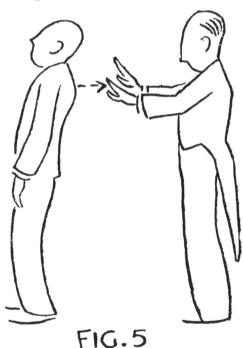

FIG. 5

As your suggestions thus continue, soon your subject will commence to sway, and will shortly topple directly over backward into your arms. As he falls, be sure and catch him, and immediately help him to regain his balance.

Explaining that this influence of ideas held in the mind affects the sense of balance in any direction concentrated upon, you ask your subject next to stand facing you, as you experiment in drawing him over forwards.

Then have him look you directly in the eyes, and as he does this, fix your own gaze directly upon the **root of his nose—looking him straight and intently between the eyes.** By your eyes being thus focused you will find that you can center your gaze much more positively and forcefully than if you were to look directly into the eyes of your subject. This bit of technique has been called by some operators, "The Hypnotic Gaze."

Next advise your subject to concentrate on your suggestions pulling him over forward, and that soon he will find himself falling forward right towards you, just as he did in falling over backward in the previous experiment. Now raise your hands and rest them very lightly on each side of his head (See Fig. 6).

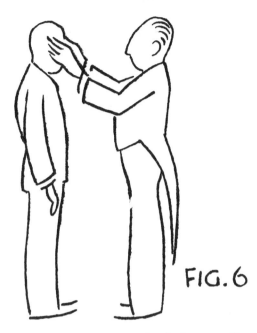

FIG. 6

Still looking him squarely between the eyes, you allow your fingers to rest thus on his temples for a few seconds in silence; and then, moving your left foot back a step, slowly and very lightly draw your fingers along the sides of his head toward the front, at the same time bending your body backwards a bit at the hips; your two hands coming together in the front of his forehead. Then, with a slow motion, separate them, and bending forward, again place your fingers upon the sides of his head and withdraw them slowly and lingeringly towards the front, ending the stroke in the center of his forehead as previously.

Having performed this forward drawing motion three times, suggest to him very slowly and impressively, while still keeping your gaze intently centered on the root of his nose and always observing carefully that his eyes do not wander from yours for even an instant, "Now you feel a drawing impulse causing you to fall forward. Do not resist; I shall catch you. Let yourself go. You are coming forward. You are falling forward right over toward me." As you give these suggestions, very slowly draw your hands again forward along the sides of his head, finally drawing them completely clear of his head as you bend backward a bit and downward . . . and your subject will follow right along and fall directly forward into your arms (See Fig. 7).

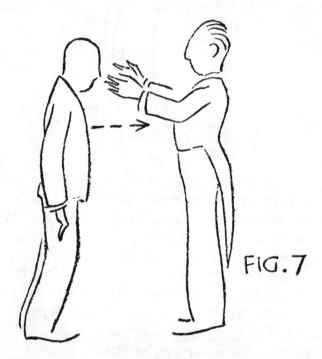

FIG. 7

Keep your suggestion going constantly in this test as, "You are falling forward. You are falling forward. You are falling forward. Now when I withdraw my hands from your temples you will fall forward—right over forward, forward, forward," and remember to constantly watch the eyes of your subject. If they remain fixed and intent you can be certain of the experiment succeeding, but if they waver from yours, stop the experiment at once as you explain that he must keep his gaze riveted upon yours in order to maintain the necessary degree of concentration for the experiment to succeed; then proceed with the test until he falls directly over into your arms, and at once again help him to regain his balance.

Since you have been discussing the William James theory of ideo-motor action, i.e., that every idea centered in the mind leads unconsciously to motor action, notice how in the present instance the **idea of falling** actually caused the subject to so fall.

The subject's reaction to the experiment is further enlightening. He knows he did not deliberately try to fall over. To him the sensation seemed exactly as if some outside force were actually drawing him, pulling on him, and causing him to fall. This sensation of an outside force develops because suggestion produces an **involuntary** rather than a voluntary affect— for in actual fact, the force that produces the subject's fall originates within his own mind, and from thence imparts automatic (unconscious) motion to his muscles, which in turn cause him to actually sway in the direction of his thought, and eventually completely fall over.

Your subject having proceeded thus far with you, and having experienced some very tangible, but in no way disturbing, effects, there is no reason why you should not now plunge directly into a little discussion of **The Power of Suggestion** and some of the interesting things that can be accomplished through its use. This little story illustrates it well:

Imagine, if you will, that we have a plank of wood, say, one foot wide and twelve feet long. We place it on the floor in this room and walk along it from one end to the other. Can you keep your balance as you do it? Easily, of course you can. All right, now let's say we take that very same plank and place it between two tall buildings. Now try and walk over it. Can you do it? Come now, why do you refuse; you just walked over that very same board only a few minutes before —yet now you say you cannot do it. Or, in the event that you choose to try, the chances are you would crawl out a little ways, get panicky, become dizzy, and soon take a disastrous fall to the street below. Why?

Because the position of the board—**now** stretched out over a great height between two tall buildings **suggests** the idea of a fall. Actually it is no more difficult to keep your balance in walking along that board in its present condition between the buildings than it was when you walked along it in the security of the room. But **the suggestion of falling** is now present, and is so powerful that it definitely interferes with your sense of balance. And, reason about it as you will—you cannot overcome that idea of a fall!

You will find that a little story such as that, clearly illustrates to your subject just what the power of suggestion is and how it operates, and puts him in a receptive mood for more advanced experiments. Another example of suggestion you can tell him is the classical illustration, frequently performed by psychologists on their classes. In this, the instructor will exhibit a glass jar containing what he calls a very delightful perfume. He tells his students of the very special nature of this perfume. How the sweet odor of the flowers has been captured and put within the essence. He then asks how they would like to smell the perfume, and requests that as promptly as they detect the odor in the room that they raise their hands.

The professor next uncorks the jar and wafts it about through the air, and soon a good 75 per cent of his class raise their hands stating that they can smell the flower scent of the perfume. Now, the remarkable part of the experiment is that in actual fact that jar contained nothing but pure water. **Of such is the power of suggestion.**

Suggestions (suggestive ideas) are ideas which when centered in the mind stimulate the imagination and lead to an active, unconscious response. The term **unconscious** response is used to describe suggestive ideas because once they go into action they produce effects **involuntarily** on the part of the subject.

You can now propose a direct experiment in suggestion to your subject.

Request your subject to again look directly into your eyes and under no circumstances to remove his gaze from yours. Now stretch your hands out towards him, palms upward, and tell him to grasp your hands tightly; as tightly as he possibly can. At the same time bend your head forward a little until it is within six inches of his own (See Fig. 8).

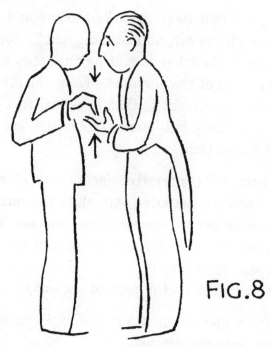

FIG.8

After maintaining this position for ten seconds or so, suggest very positively and slowly, "You cannot unclasp your hands. You cannot take them away from mine. They are fastened to mine and you cannot move them. You will find the muscles of your arms and hands are rigid and tight. Stuck tight! Try and take your hands away. Try hard, but you cannot!"

If your subject is following your suggestions with earnest concentration his hands will become tightly locked to yours. He will pull and struggle and be entirely unable to release his grip. **You can tell by his eyes how intently he is concentrating on your suggestions.** His gaze must be fixed and earnest, and when the suggestions are being accepted and he starts to pull and yet finds that his hands continue to cling to yours, you will note a little puzzled expression creep into his eyes. Hammer home your suggestions even more forcefully at this point, "See, your hands are stuck, they are stuck so tightly to mine that you cannot pull them away try as hard as you will. Try, try hard! They will not come free . . . they are stuck, stuck tight!"

After your subject has tried in vain to release his hands from yours for a few seconds, say, "All right now, Relax! Relax your hands. You can now release them. Your hands are free!" And your subject will be able to immediately unlock his grip.

The successful induction of this experiment requires a deeper degree of concentration than the previous test influencing the sense of balance. In your experimenting be certain to use the three preliminary tests given in this chapter in the order presented, as they have been arranged for ease of execution, **and succeed completely with each test you work with your subject before carrying on to the next.**

We come now to a most intriguing phase of hypnotic influence which you should master thoroughly as these experiments will prove most valuable to your ultimate stage work.

EXPERIMENTS IN THE WAKING STATE

Many students of Hypnotism seem surprised to learn that it is possible to produce very striking hypnotic effects in the waking state, entirely independent of the trance. Basically, suggestive influence in the waking state is not different from suggestive influence in the hypnotic state except in degree of intensity; further, these tests in the waking state have the advantage of gradually "conditioning" your subject (or subjects) for the more advanced hypnotic experiments yet to come.

If you have succeeded in effectively fastening your subject's hands to yours as described in the last chapter, you are now ready for this next test which is undoubtedly the most important of any you have performed thus far. If you succeed in this experiment, you can be almost certain of success in all manner of waking hypnotic effects of the muscular variety. Indeed, response to this test can often be used as a means of grading a subject's response to suggestion and his capacity as a good hypnotic subject.

Locking the Hands Together

Have your subject stand facing you and again look directly into your eyes and under no circumstances to remove his gaze. Then request him to extend his arms out straight in front of him, to clasp his hands together and interlock the fingers. Ask him to push his hands as tightly together as he possibly can, to make his arms stiff and rigid, and to think he cannot take his hands apart by repeating over and over mentally the words, "I can't get my hands apart, I can't get them apart, I can't get them apart."

Now stretch out your hands towards him and clasp his locked hand in yours pressing on them firmly yet gently. Keep your eyes fixed on him, focusing directly at the root of his nose, never removing your gaze at any time. And watch your subject's eyes. If they remain fixed and centered then he is concentrating as directed, but if they waver and shift, command him not to look away, and to keep his gaze firm and steady as he concentrates on the suggestions (See Fig. 9).

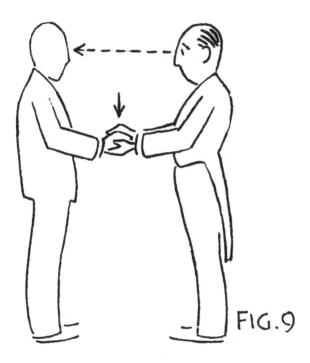

FIG. 9

Now say to the subject in a positive tone, "You will find your hands are sticking together tight, tighter, tighter, tight, and you cannot take them apart. You cannot unclasp your hands, they are stuck tightly together, they will not come apart, they are stuck tight, tight, tight!" As you give these suggestions continue pressing on your subject's clasped hands, clasping them, pressing them tighter and tighter together. Now, remove your hands, giving the subject a chance to test the influence as you continue. "You will find the muscles of your arms and hands are so rigid and stiff that your hands simply will not come apart. They are stuck tight together, stuck tight! Try and take your hands apart. Try hard. PULL! Pull with all of your might! They will not come, they are stuck tight together."

If your subject has been following your suggestions with earnest concentration, his hands will have become so tightly locked together that tug and struggle as he will he simply cannot pull his locked hands apart.

In giving these suggestions, remember to speak positively slowly, and distinctly, becoming continuously more and more forceful . . . and throw more and more energy in subsequent suggestions until the climax is reached when the subject is told that he cannot take his hands apart.

As soon as your subject has tried in vain to release his hands, snap your fingers beside his ear and suggest, "All right now, it's all gone. Relax, you can take your hands apart now." Immediately, the concentration being broken, he will find that he can now separate his hands.

Occasionally the subject's hands will have become so tightly locked together that they will not separate even when you tell him to now relax and take them apart. In such a case, simply take them gently in your own hands and softly suggest, "All right now, relax,

relax your hands. I will count slowly from one to three, and at the count of 'three' your hands will come right apart." Then count, "One, two, three," and at the count of "three," suddenly clap your hands together, and his hands will then easily separate. (See Fig. 10.)

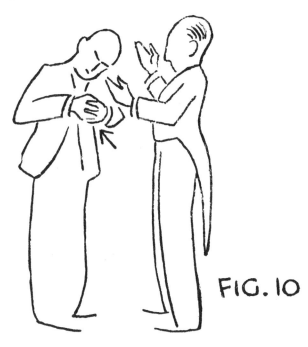

FIG. 10

Stiffening the Leg

Ask your subject to place his weight on his left leg, while you take hold of his right hand. Tell him to look you straight in the eyes, and to hold the idea firmly in his mind that he will be unable to bend his leg. And impress on him that his eyes must follow yours under all conditions.

Now make a few passes down his leg with your hands commencing about six inches above the knee, and press in slightly on the knee joint. While making

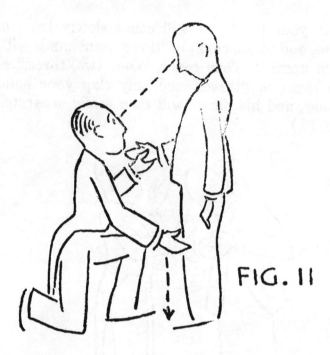

FIG. 11

these passes, say positively, "Now you will find your leg is getting stiff—stiff—stiffer—stiffer—stiff—and you cannot bend it. The knee joint is getting so stiff you cannot bend it. You can feel your muscles getting more and more rigid. It is impossible for you to bend your leg; it is stiff, stiff, stiff. Try to bend it. You can't do it. Try, try hard!" As you say these last words, rise up slowly, keeping your gaze centered at the root of your subject's nose between the eyes, and pull him toward you actually causing him to walk stiff-legged.

When he has walked some ten or twelve feet on his stiff leg, remove the influence by striking your hands together as you say, "All right, it is all gone now, you can bend your leg now, it is all loose and free."

Stiffening the Arm

The process is similar to that of stiffening the leg. Have the subject close his hand into a tight fist, and make his arm very stiff as he holds it stretched out straight in front of himself. Now take hold of his fist and make a few passes down the inside of his arm as you suggest, "Your arm is getting stiff, stiff, stiffer, stiffer, stiff. You cannot bend it. Try hard, it is so stiff, and the harder you try to bend it, the stiffer it becomes. See you cannot bend it." Remove the effect again by the clapping of your hands and the suggestions of "Relax now, it is all gone. Relax your arm."

In giving all of these tests in the waking state, make certain that your subject's gaze is always intent upon you. You will find that as you proceed from test to test, and that as your subject continues to respond to each, that you may conduct each test more and more rapidly, until often just a very few sharp suggestive commands will obtain the desired results.

Inability to Speak

Have your subject seated in front of you, staring directly into your eyes, and when you notice his pupils become set, begin stroking down the sides of his face and around the mouth gently as you suggest, "The muscles about your mouth are becoming set. Your lips are becoming stuck fast together. The muscles are so stiff you cannot open your mouth; it is stuck fast, fast. You can't open your mouth. It is impossible for you to open it. You can't even tell me what your name is. Try, try hard! Tell me your name if you can. See you cannot even speak your own name."

Your subject will strive to speak, but his mouth remains tightly shut. Then move your fingers gently around his cheeks and suggest, "Now your mouth muscles are relaxing and you can speak, but you still cannot speak your name." Suddenly place the forefinger of your right hand directly in the center of his forehead as you positively state, "In fact, you cannot even remember your own name. See you can speak, say 'Hello' to me (Subject says, 'Hello'), but you cannot speak your own name, you can't even remember it, can you!"

Watch your subject's eyes and you will see a peculiar blank expression creep into them, then suggest, "I'll tell you what your name is, it is Oswald Dinglehoffer (or some humorous name). It is Oswald Dinglehoffer. Your name is Oswald Dinglehoffer! All right, say your name now. It is Oswald Dinglehoffer! What is your name? . . . SAY IT!"

If your suggestions have been given with sufficient positive assurance, paced at almost a staccato pressure your subject will suddenly blurt out, "Oswald Dinglehoffer!" Immediately clap your hands and say, "All right, it is all gone now. You can remember your real name. What is your name?" Your subject states his name.

Fastening a Stick to the Hands

Have your subject stand before you and tightly grip a broom handle or a cane; ask him to look into your eyes and to grasp the stick tightly—fingers below, thumbs on top; tell him to think that he cannot let go of the stick, and that he will find, when you count "Three," that his hands are stuck tightly to it (See Fig. 12); that he cannot throw it down, and the more he tries the tighter it will stick to his hands. Then say, "Ready. One—two—three! Now you cannot throw the stick down. Try. Try hard! You cannot throw it down; the more you try, the more it sticks to your hands." Suddenly clap your hands and say, "All right, you can let go of it now. Throw it!" And your subject will throw the stick from him with vengeance.

FIG. 12

Unable to Sit Down

Have the subject stand in front of a chair which is placed directly behind him. He looks, as always, directly into your eyes, and you request him to make his legs perfectly stiff and to think that he cannot sit down; that when you count "Three" he will find that his legs are stiff and rigid, and that he cannot sit down, and that the more he tries, the stiffer his legs will become. Then suggest, "Ready. One, two, three —now you cannot sit down. Your legs are stiff, you cannot sit down. Try to sit down, try hard, but you cannot!"

After the subject has tried for a few seconds, remove the influence by clapping your hands quickly and saying, "All right, it's all gone now—you can now sit down. It's all gone."

Unable to Stand Up

Have the subject sit in a chair and look in your eyes as you suggest, "You are getting stuck in that chair. You're glued to the seat. Think hard on how stiff your muscles are; how stuck you are to the seat of that chair. You can't get up—you are stuck to it. I will count from one to three, at the count of three you will find you cannot rise out of that chair no matter how hard you may try. You are stuck tight to the seat of that chair. Ready. One, two, three. See, you are stuck! You try to get up, but you can't! Try and get up!"

After the subject has tried in vain to rise, suddenly clap your hands and say, "All right now, get up. You can rise now. It's all gone!" and the subject gingerly arises and looks quizzically at the seat of his chair.

If you have succeeded in these tests you can readily influence your subject in all such types of muscular-suggestive experiments, which can be most numerous. A little imagination will readily give you numerous effective experiments which you can try. For example, you can fasten your subject's mouth open so he cannot close it; you can place his hand flat on the floor so that it is impossible for him to pull it free; you can stick his feet in position so that he cannot walk. In all of these tests the principle and application is mainly the same, i.e., to fix the subject's attention acutely on you by having him look directly into your eyes, while you gaze at him directly between the eyes at the root of his nose, while he concentrates on the barrage of suggestions which you hammer home into his mind by positive repetition of the various effects you wish to accomplish.

Unless a person has observed or experienced the influence of suggestion himself, it is hard to realize through a description on paper just how worded commands, such as these, can produce such effects. You must remember that it is not the words that are important but rather the ideas they convey, and that the response of the subject to these ideas is not a voluntary thing; the action being entirely involuntary on the part of your subject as your train of suggestions take hold of the unconscious side of his personality and direct its responses quite independent of his will. To illustrate this point, suppose we again recall the incident of trying to walk over that board stretched out between two tall buildings. We tried in vain to counteract our fear of a fall in walking over the board, and **the more we tried not to fall, the more we felt that surely we would fall.**

Or, consider the case of a man obsessed by stage-fright. He fears that he may get tongue-tied and be unable to speak, so he reasons and reasons with himself that he has nothing to fear, that talking to a large group is no harder than talking before one person, and that he will be able to talk clearly and freely before his audience. Yet, comes the time for his speech and the suggestive idea of the fear that he cannot speak (Imagination) completely eclipses his reasoning that he can (Will), and he becomes tongue-tied, blunders about, and develops an amazing case of stage-fright.

Which brings us to one of the basic laws in the operation of suggestion: **When the Imagination and the Will are in conflict, the Imagination invariably wins.**

You can well begin to see the power that does exist in suggestive ideas. Illustrations of its operation lie about us continually—selling and advertising are excellent examples. These constantly endeavor to appeal to our emotions, to stimulate our imaginations, and implant a desire for the product. And when successful, the purchase, or culmination of our aroused desire, becomes a purely **automatic process.** Fortunately for us, all suggestive ideas do not take root in our minds. If they did life would be a very complicated place indeed, and we would be buffeted about constantly from one suggestion to another without a vestige of will of our own. For in actual fact, ninety-nine out of a hundred of the ideas that are presented to us do not carry enough of **an emotional wallop to stimulate our imagination to the extent that they become sufficiently centered in our attention to give rise to unconscious (automatic) effects . . . or else they are defeated by counter-suggestions already in force in our minds.** Obviously, the vast majority of suggestions we reject, or else keep purely within the realm of reason. That is where your skill as a Hypnotist must come in; for you must give your suggestions in such a manner that they will tend to arouse an emotional response and spark the imagination.

Some people are quite resistant to the effects of suggestion, so naturally you cannot expect to influence every person you experiment on, especially at the very beginning of your training period. But that is the very purpose of your practice. Quite possibly you may influence and hypnotize the very first person you work with, or you may fail with the first dozen or more, but consider it all under the heading of experience and perseverance. Simply be courteous and never show any disappointment at failure. If you have difficulty, merely remark that it isn't possible to hypnotize everyone at the very first trial, and proceed on with your work. There is a knack in giving suggestions so that they will produce hypnotic effects which come only from practice and experience. Patience and perseverance will bring this. Sooner or later you will succeed in hypnotizing someone, **and that very first subject is a very important milestone in your progress as a Hypnotist;** you will be amazed at the insight it gives you towards the successful skill of giving suggestions that hypnotize. And here's a very important little tip to keep in mind when you give such suggestions:

When you state, as an example, that your subject's hands are fastened so tightly together that he cannot pull them apart; in your own mind visualize the image of his hands being so locked together and him pulling vainly to separate them. Don't have the slightest doubt in your mind but that the experiment will occur exactly as you command it. Forget all ideas of failure. KNOW that your suggestions will be followed—such conviction does wonders to your manner, tone, and delivery in the producing of positive suggestions that automatically demand acceptance.

Suggestions given in the waking state can also influence our sensory system to some degree. Here are a couple of interesting experiments that you can try, not only on one subject but on an entire audience if you choose. They serve excellently to graphically illustrate some of the basic thoughts behind hypnotic suggestion.

The Taste Test

Hold up your right forefinger, look at it intently, and ask your subject, or those in the audience, to do likewise—raising their right forefinger up in front of their eyes. Now ask them to imagine that there is a coating of sweet sugar beginning to cover the tip of that finger, and suggest, "It is so sweet, that sugar.

So very, very sweet. That fingertip will taste so very, very sweet." Then ask them to touch the tip of their finger to the tip of their tongue and note the sweetish taste. This they do, and everyone will experience the illusion.

Now have them again look at their finger and suggest, "Your finger is no longer coated with sugar, now it is covered with salt—it is covered with grains of salt. How salty it will taste. So salty! Taste that salt." On again sampling the fingertip, sure enough a decided salty flavor can be noted.

Itchy Sensations Test

Request your subject, group of subjects, or the audience, as the case may be, to relax back in their chairs, to place their feet flat on the floor, their hands comfortably in their laps, and to think intently of the thoughts you are going to present. Then suggest: "As you sit there, thus relaxed, a most curious sensation is soon going to pass over all of you, and in a very few moments you will begin to feel an itching of the skin on various parts of your bodies. In fact, this itching sensation will soon grow so strong that you will have a decided inclination to scratch your itching skin; go right ahead, for we shall all be doing the same thing!"

As you talk thus, occasionally scratch your own shoulders and arms naturally. Be very careful that you do this in a serious manner, so that in no way you divert the audience's attention from your suggestive words. **Rather let this pantomime emphasize the verbal suggestions.**

"Now the itching is upon you. Your body itches in various places; some of you will find that your legs itch; some feel a teasing sensation to scratch the arms; others, their shoulders and other parts of the body.

"Your itching skin must be scratched to satisfy that itch; there are itches between your shoulders—do you feel them? There are itches on your shoulder blades, itches on the back, itches everywhere—itches that simply must be scratched. Go ahead, scratch your itching body. Get that enjoyable relief. How many different places on your itching skin itches now? See if you can count them to yourself."

Pause for a moment now, **to let the suggestions sink home,** while you continue with a bit of pantomime on your own itches. Then continue.

"Your body itches are perfectly normal itches. But, my, how they do itch! That's it, go ahead and scratch. Get that pleasant relief. Think of just one of the spots that seems to be itching the most upon your body. It's teasing, you want to scratch—why not? Go ahead—it brings such pleasant relief."

By this time you will have many in your audience started—scratching itches that mentally exist. Follow right on with a similar line of suggestions, and soon you will have the entire group responding to the itches. Having produced the desired effects, for the test's conclusion suggest.

"The itches are all subsiding now; all going away. Your skin feels again all pleasant, cool, and refreshed. Every itch is gone, and you feel good all over. Just swell!"

Does this test work? How many times did you scratch yourself while reading these directions?

By this time, you have proceeded far enough with your subject so that you can very shortly propose an actual experiment in the induction of the hypnotic trance, so as a direct lead-up try this test:

Fastening the Eyelids Together

Ask your subject to be seated, and standing in front of him and a little to one side, tell him to raise his eyes to yours and look fixedly at you. When he has looked in this manner for approximately ten seconds, gently close his eyes with your fingertips, and resting your other hand on his pulse, tell him to continue to look upward underneath his closed lids (See Fig. 13).

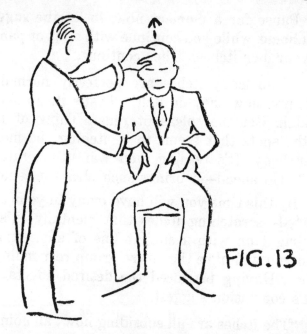

FIG. 13

Now say to him very slowly and impressively. "Your eyes are becoming stuck together. The lids are stuck tight. They will not open . Your eyes are stuck shut. You cannot open your eyes—try as you will you cannot open them. Try hard. Hard! See, they are stuck tight—they will not open. They are stuck tight —glued shut." As you give these suggestions, place the thumb of your right hand on the subject's forehead just above the bridge of his nose and press downward.

Your subject will in vain struggle and try to open his eyes, but he simply cannot. His eyebrows will rise and fall, but the eyelids will remain tightly shut. Having made several ineffectual attempts to open them, suddenly remove your thumb from the center of his forehead, snap your fingers by his ear, and say, "All right, it's all gone . . . you can open your eyes now." And his eyes will pop open with a surprised expression.

Step by step, you and your subject have thus practiced the effects of suggestion on the mind, and you are now both ready to try for complete hypnosis.

HOW TO HYPNOTIZE

So far all of your experiments have been conducted in the waking state. We are now ready to deal with an **unconscious** phase of mind. So begin by developing a few mutual understandings regarding Hypnotism between yourself and your subject.

First, explain to him that he need have no fear whatsoever of the hypnotic state, that it will be a completely harmless experience that he will thoroughly enjoy, and that the concentrated relaxation produced will actually do him a great deal of good. Then ask if he is perfectly willing to be hypnotized and advise that he must concentrate his entire attention upon all of your suggestions. Tell him not to resist, to just let himself go, and willingly place himself in your hands with confidence as you conduct this experiment in Hypnotism together.

These pre-trance understandings are most important, for to make the experiment a success there must exist a feeling of confidence, trust, and co-operation between the subject and the Hypnotist.

Having acquired this initial understanding, explain to your subject that he is not to wonder whether or not he will go to sleep, but is to just relax his mind and let himself drift gently into a passive, drowsy state as he concentrates on your suggestions.

Now get your HYPNODISK. This device you have prepared in advance by carefully tracing Fig. 14 on a piece of cardboard and filling it in with black drawing ink, or having an artist reproduce it for you. Cut around the outside circle and you have the HYPNODISK.

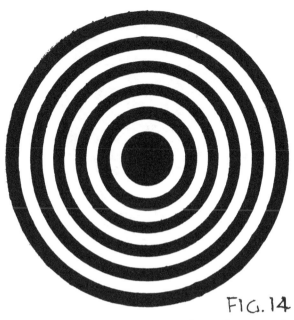

FIG. 14

In using it, the DISK is held at the rear between your thumb and fingers, and with a rotating motion of the hand is revolved around and around in a small three- or four-inch circle (See Fig. 15). Hold the disk up in front of your subject in a position that will make his eyes strain upward a bit to look at it (See Fig. 16). Continue this rotating motion until the eyes of your subject close, and remain closed; then place the DISK aside.

Let us continue on now with our experiment in hypnotizing.

Your subject prepared to go to sleep in the hypnotic trance, ask him to take a seat in a comfortable chair, and to relax well back. Have him adjust himself so he will be completely comfortable and will not have to move about. Then hold the HYPNODISK six or seven inches in front of his eyes, asking him to watch it closely, allowing his eyes to follow its rotary

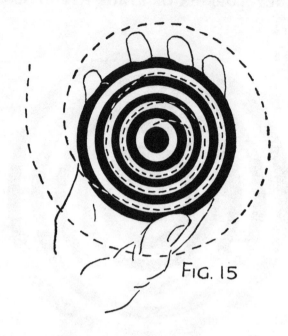

FIG. 15

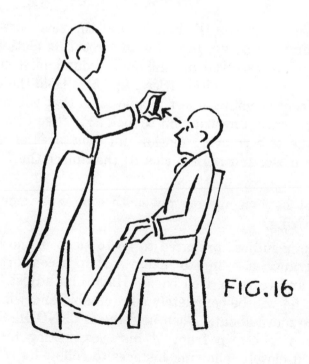

FIG. 16

motions, and to think of sleep.

You then continue rotating the DISK around and around for four or five minutes, until your subject's eyes close. And while revolving the DISK, repeat the following suggestions in a low, monotonous, but positive tone of voice:

"Your eyelids feel heavy. Your eyes are getting tired—they are getting moist—they are beginning to wink. You cannot see distinctly any longer. Your eyelids are closing." Repeat these suggestions over and over as many times as is necessary to close your subject's eyes. In the event that his eyes do not close after a reasonable time, directly request, "Close your eyes tightly now and go sound asleep."

Next place your hands on the subject's head so your thumbs rest together in the center of his forehead just above the eyes and your fingers lie along each side of his head (See 17). Now move your thumbs slowly from the center of the forehead outward over the temples in a gentle stroking motion, and repeat this process for two or three minutes. Keep your fingers still, just moving the thumbs, as you say, "Sleep—sleepy—sleepy—sleepy—sleep — sound sleep—sleep—sleepy—sleep." Speak in a slow, positive monotonous tone.

Next place the fingers of your left hand on the top of the subject's head, with the thumb of the hand resting on his temple. Leave the fingers of your right hand resting along side of the subject's head just as they were at first, and place the right thumb in the center of his forehead immediately under the hair line. Move this thumb down from his hair line over the center of his forehead slowly until it reaches a little below the bridge of his nose. Vary these stroking motions of your right thumb occasionally by stroking all

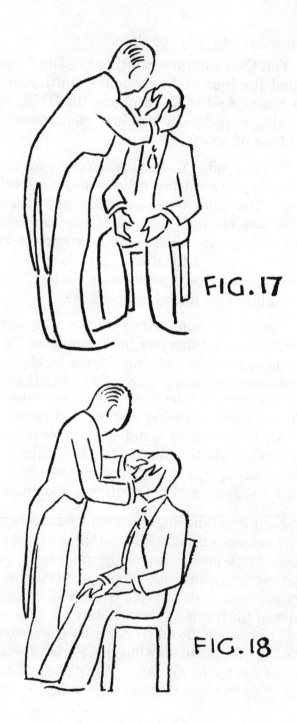

FIG. 17

FIG. 18

the way down to the tip of the nose. In making these thumb strokes keep the fingers still. Repeat the process of moving the thumb down the center of the subject's forehead for three or four minutes, and during the entire process continue on giving suggestions of, "Sleep—sleepy—sleep—sleep—etc." (See Fig. 18.)

Now move your left thumb from the subject's temple to the root of his nose, between the eyes, leaving the fingers still resting on top of his head, and with your right hand begin to stroke downward over his hair from the back part of the top of the subject's head on down to the base of his brain (See Fig. 19). Make these passes slowly, using a firm pressure—all the time continuing to give suggestions of, "Sleep—sound asleep——deep, deep sleep." Continue these downward passes over the back of the head for three or four minutes.

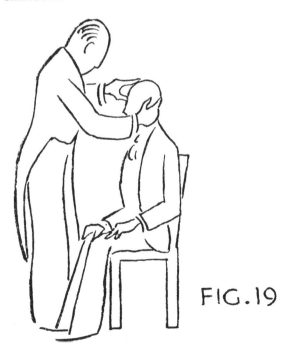

FIG. 19

Standing on the right side of your subject with your left hand still resting in its previous position on his head (See Fig. 20) repeat the following "sleep formula" in low, positive, monotonous tones (let the monotony of your voice be like the ticking of a clock), "Your eyes are closed tightly—you cannot open them. your arms feel heavy. Your hands are motionless. You cannot move. You cannot feel anything. Everything is dark to you. You are going sound asleep—sleep—sleepy—sleepy—sleep — sound asleep — sound asleep—sound asleep—your head feels heavy—your limbs feel like lead—you are so sleepy—when I count three you will go into a deep, deep sleep. One, two, three. You are sound asleep."

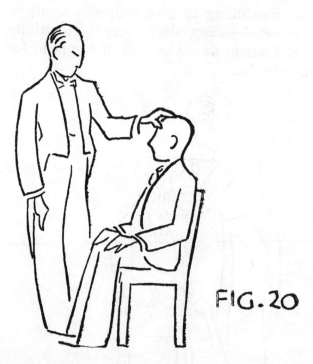

FIG. 20

Now start at the first of this "sleep formula" and repeat it again, and continue this process of repetition over and over for five minutes or so. Occasionally, you can continue it to advantage for as long as ten or even fifteen minutes.

By the end of thirty minutes, at the very most, from the time of your starting to hypnotize, if your subject is not yet asleep discontinue the work for that day and try it again at a later period.

Now, the method of hypnotizing just described is unquestionably long, slow, and somewhat tedious, but since you are still in an apprentice period of learning the art, it is a wise one to first apply, as with it you will find that you can influence a great many of the subjects on whom you practice.

As you develop skill in your work, many of your subjects will go to sleep in but a few minutes, in which case you can discontinue the long process of repeating the "sleep formula" over and over. And as your results continue to improve, of course the length of time you give to each successive step in the process may be shortened until this method of inducing hypnosis need not occupy more than four to six minutes. However, when first learning to hypnotize, it is well to work slowly and thoroughly, as such will not only teach you more, but will assure you a greater percentage of successes in completely inducing the hypnotic sleep.

A VARIETY OF HYPNOTIC METHODS

In this chapter we shall discuss some further methods of hypnotizing. You will find these very valuable additions to your knowledge as they will equip you with four very fine techniques of inducing the hypnotic trance.

The Sidney Flower Method

This process will be found useful in affecting people who find it difficult to concentrate their attention upon the idea of sleep as applied in the previous chapter. The essential thing about Mr. Flower's method is that while the operator counts, the subject opens and closes his eyes, keeping time with the counting.

Have your subject seat himself in a comfortable position, and explain to him that you want him to go to sleep. After he has become perfectly passive, have him look directly into your eyes, while you gaze intently at the root of his nose.

Now tell him that you are going to count to him slowly, and that as you say each number you wish him to close his eyes . . . then to open them and be ready to close them again by the time you say, the next number. For instance, you slowly count, "One, two, three, four." At each count the subject is to close his eyes and open them in between. He is to keep his eyes focused on yours at all times, though, even when they are closed.

Start counting now slowly and in rhythm, and you will find that as you continue the counting that the period during which the subject's eyes remain open becomes shorter and shorter, and finally, instead of the eyes opening, there will probably be only a movement of the eyebrows. (See Fig. 21.)

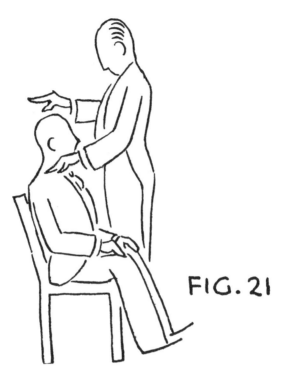

FIG. 21

Many subjects will go to sleep under this method by the time you have counted fifteen or twenty, and it is rarely necessary to count over one hundred. When you find the eyes are closed, and the subject does not seem able to open them, instead of continuing with the counting begin to say (**and be sure you do** not change the rhythm of your previous tone), "Sleep. Sleep. Sleepy. Sleepy. Sleep. You—are—going—to—sleep. Fast—fast—asleep. Asleep. Sleep. Sleepy. Sleep. Etc."

Soon the subject's head will drop forward, and you will notice he is very drowsy. At this point you can commence some of the head stroking passes, as previously explained, while you suggest the "sleep formula" to your subject.

Now, in this method very little verbal suggestion is used, so as you proceed with the technique keep your gaze fixed on the top of his head and concentrate intently on the subject getting drowsy, and finally that he is going soundly to sleep. Whatever the stages in the induction of hypnotic sleep you wish to develop in your subject—relaxation, heaviness of limbs, drowsiness, sleep—think of these mentally to yourself, **suggesting them mentally to your subject.** In other words, give your suggestion to your subject just as you would verbally, but don't speak them—THINK THEM.

Next hold your hand in front of the subject's closed eyes, about two inches from his face, casting a dark shadow over them. This shadow is held for a short time, and is suddenly removed. The effect of this is to bring to the closed eyes a sensation of darkness that quickly changes again to diffused redness. Again repeat the shadow effect: pulling it suddenly away. By drawing the hands off to each side of the face the shadow will pass in that direction. By drawing the hands past the eyes in an upward direction, the shadow will follow accordingly. (See Fig. 22.) Vary the process, but always keep the effect of shadow to light, shadow to light following a definite pattern in rhythm. Continue this process for about three minutes. With many subjects this method of inducing the trance will be found to work very rapidly.

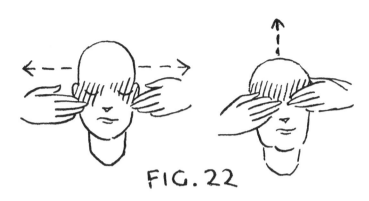

FIG. 22

The Dwight Salisbury Method

In this rather unusual technique the subject is comfortably seated in front of a bright light which shines directly into his eyes. To spare him from the light he is requested to close his eyelids. Use as bright a light as you can secure, and place it at such a level that the subject has to look up to it, which will necessitate his leaning his head back so that the muscles of the neck will be drawn tight and taut.

If you will experiment a bit with this yourself, you will find that even though the eyelids are tightly shut, the light can still be plainly noticed as a sort of reddish glare as it penetrates through the closed lids. So prepared, take up a position directly to the rear of your subject, and bend your head in low so that you are breathing directly upon either the top of the head or the forehead of the subject. (See Fig. 23.)

Then gently, very gently, make passes over the face of your subject, occasionally touching his cheeks lightly here and there. Rub the forehead softly, and then continue with more of the non-contact shadow passes in front of his face. Sometimes open the fingers of your hands as you pass them in front of the closed eyes; this produces a flickering effect. This flickering

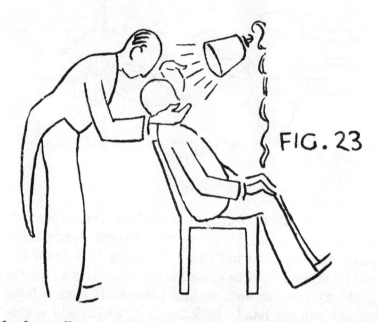

FIG. 23

shadow effect is decidedly hypnotic. Then again close the fingers and make the shadow solid and black. Sometimes use just one hand in making the shadow, and sometimes both. Make passes now over the body of the subject going from the face as far down as the stomach. Then make passes down over the shoulders and chest, sometimes touching lightly, and sometimes without contact.

As you continue with this process, you will notice that your subject will develop a marked quivering of the eyelids, and that the head will frequently fall forward on the chest or shoulder; you can assist this by gently pushing it forward on the opposite side from which you wish it to fall. The muscles of the mouth will also become somewhat drawn, and the breathing deepens and quickens.

Your subject's head having fallen forward on his chest and his breathing having become deep and regular, turn out the light, and softly, so softly that your voice is barely a whisper that can be heard only by the subject, commence giving your "sleep formula" of verbal suggestions.

Next make short passes with contact down the arms, and press upon the shoulders as you continue to increase the depth of the trance.

This method will be found very useful in working with nervous persons; it is not tiring to the subject and is very soothing. Being highly esthetic and genteel, it can be especially recommended for hypnotizing women.

The Herbert Flint Method

Have your subject stand, directly facing you, and ask him to look into your eyes as you fasten your own gaze on the root of his nose.

Then place your hands on his shoulders, and in a tone of positive authority say, "I am going to put you deeply asleep. I want you to relax. Your body will grow very light; you can feel it! You must feel it for you are going to sleep! You cannot help yourself! You are going to sleep! Deep asleep!"

Now begin to rock his body gently to and from you—**very easy and slowly** (See Fig. 24). Continue your positive barrage of suggestions that he is going to sleep! That he cannot help himself for he is going fast asleep! That his eyelids are heavy and must close! Then command forcefully, "CLOSE YOUR EYES!" Next place your fingers over his closed eyes and repeat, "Deep asleep! Sleep! Deep asleep! Nothing will awaken you until I command you to awaken! You are sound asleep!"

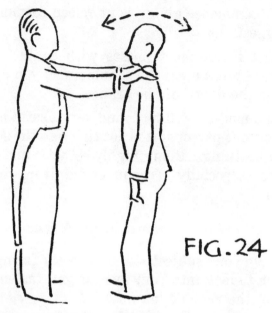

FIG. 24

This is a method developed essentially by a stage operator, and embodies a COMMAND approach in the giving of suggestions. Except under conditions of the stage, or in a situation where belief is already aroused in the performer's powers, such a process can hardly be recommended. However, some subjects do seem to respond better to the command approach than to the persuasive. Such a method is decidedly worthwhile knowing, as when the conditions are right it can throw many subjects very quickly into hypnosis.

The basic psychology behind the command approach is the subject's **fear** of the performer's ability to hypnotize him. A person with such a complex will frequently be encountered, and can be easily recognized by the shy, docile characteristics of his personality coupled with a definite air of self-consciousness. The extent to which some operators have taken advantage of such situations is excellently described by Colin Bennett.

"Seizing upon a youth who had been reduced to the right state of moral funk, the Hypnotist would catch him by the shoulders and pull him swiftly to his feet, clapping his left hand round the back of the youth's head. With the right hand he would hold him equally firmly and, it seemed to the frightened lad, menacingly by the point of the jaw, gaze hard into the youth's eyes and give the peremptory order 'SLEEP!'

"One American stage Hypnotist, who also toured successfully in this country, was not content with this degree of forcefulness. His way was to collar the most sheepish-looking youth as above and bombard him Coué-fashion with a rapid and deliberately threatening repetition of the formula, 'Sleep! What d'ye mean? What d'ye mean, I say? Sleep, I tell ye, Sleep! What d'ye mean? What d'ye mean?'

"The extraordinary question, thus repeated in an explosive whisper often had so shattering an effect upon the volunteer subject that his funk turned into hypnosis there and then."

While the command approach can occasionally be used effectively to induce the hypnotic trance, extreme measures such as these cited by Mr. Bennett can certainly never be condoned. They belong to another age; no more to be compared with the gentlemanly style of the modern hypnotist than is grandpa's one-horse shay to the streamlined cars of today.

The Ormond McGill Method

For most general practice this method will be found highly effective. It offers something of an innovation in hypnotic techniques.

Have your subject take a seat in a comfortable chair and relax back. Take a position about two feet in front of him and request that he look directly into your **right eye,** indicating the eye into which he is to stare with a gesture of your hand.

And you in turn gaze back at him, focusing your gaze directly upon his right eye. Tell him not to let his gaze wander under any conditions, and to concentrate intently upon every thought you give him. (See Fig. 25.)

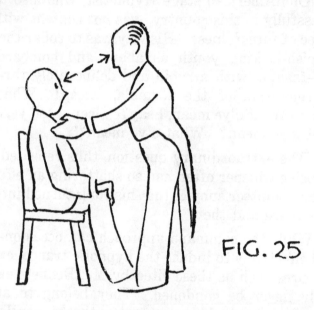

FIG. 25

Now, the underlying secrets that make this method so unusual and so productive of positive results are that in its process **the operator mildly hypnotizes himself as he entrances his subject.** Thus he feels and experiences the same sensations that his subject is experiencing, and since **the method employs a progressive series of hypnotic suggestions** that takes the subject along, sensation by sensation, through the various stages of relaxation on down to deep sleep, **the operator is enabled to exactly time the giving of the proper suggestions.**

Secondly, this process tends to place the hypnotist more readily **en rapport with his subject,** and as he presents each suggestion **he firmly concentrates upon it, in his own mind visualizing that he is projecting the sensation-idea right along with the suggestive-words to his subject.** Since he is experiencing the sensation induced by the suggestions, himself; this is readily done. In actual practice, the process works like this by example:

In the course of your suggestion series, let us say, you have come to the point where the eyes are becoming heavy and fatigued. You experience the sensation of burning in your own eyes, so you know that when you utter the suggestions, "Your eyes are heavy and tired. How they burn. How badly you want to close them. You simply must close them," that your subject is exactly experiencing those very same sensations. And, as you present those suggestions not only do you say the words; but, at the same time, you earnestly concentrate your mind on the idea of your subject's eyes getting tired, heavy and burning. **Do this by visualizing a picture of his eyes becoming so fatigued.** Thus, step by step, you mentally visualize your suggestions as you apply this method. Understanding now the introspective aspects of the process, your subject seated comfortably relaxed before you, staring into your eye as you stare back into his, you are ready to proceed.

Suggest to your subject, "As you look into my eye you will begin to feel a most pleasant calm creeping over you, as you relax all of the muscles of your body. Relax the muscles of your head and face, right on down through the muscles of your neck and shoulders. Every muscle relaxing through your entire body, right on down to your feet. You are becoming so relaxed and calm. All is so quiet and calm. It's just like a heavy, dark cloak being draped about and over your body. All is so quiet and calm."

As you give your suggestions make short gentle passes downward in the direction of your subject. Perform these in a sort of downward ellipse, starting with both hands in near your face, then bringing the hands out and downward towards your subject, and completing the elongated circle by bringing your hands back again towards your face (See Fig. 26). Make these passes rather unobtrusive, more to emphasize your subject's attention to your eyes and suggestions than to cause notice of themselves.

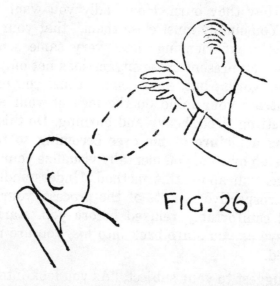

FIG. 26

Proceed with your suggestions, "And your eyes are getting fixed, set upon mine." **As you say this, make a gesture from his eye towards yours.** "And how tired your eyes are becoming. The lids are getting so heavy that they just want to blink and close: How you want to close those tired eyes. But, they won't close yet because they are set, looking directly into my eye. How your eyes burn and smart. How you want to close them, they are so heavy, so tired. How badly those eyes burn and want to close. All right, let them close. I will count slowly from one to ten. With every count your eyes will get heavier and heavier, until by the time I reach ten, or before, they will be tightly closed. All right now—one, two—your eyes are getting heavy, they are beginning to close. Three. How heavy your eyes are. The upper lids are pulling down and the lower lids are drawing up. Your eyes are closing. How heavy they are. Close them tight. Four. Five. Let your tired eyes close. They are so heavy and tired. Close your eyes. Six. Seven. That's it, close those tired eyes. Eight. Nine. Ten. Eyes closed all down tightly now. Tight!"

Time the giving of these suggestions to the manner in which your eyes feel, and by the reactions of your subject as his eyelids wink, blink, and droop. By the time you reach the count of "Ten," his eyes should be tighty closed. If they are not, then gently close the lids with your fingertips as you suggest, "Close those tired eyes now, and let them rest." Then continue,

"Oh, how good it feels to close those tired eyes. They are so tired, it feels so good to let them rest. How tightly shut they are . . . shutting tighter and tighter. They are getting stuck together. They just won't open any more. They are stuck shut together . . . stuck tight." **Place your right thumb in the center of your subject's forehead and push down toward the root of his nose, gripping, at the same time his right wrist in your left hand.** "You cannot open them, for they are stuck. They are fastened tightly together, see how they stick. Try and open them, but you cannot."

Here your subject will try in vain to open his eyes;

the eyebrows will rise and fall, but the lids will remain solidly shut. After the subject has tried for a second or two follow on,

"That's all right, just forget all about your eyes . . . just rest, now and go to sleep. Just rest and go sound asleep. Sound, sound asleep. My, how calm and relaxed you do feel . . . just calm and relaxed all over." sleep."

Now step behind your subject and gently make stroking passes over his forehead, from the center outward towards the temples (See Fig. 27), and continue to suggest, "Everything is so quiet and calm. You are getting so drowsy and sleepy. Go sound asleep. Everything is fading away. You are going to sleep. Down deep asleep. Down, down, deep asleep. Things are all getting farther and farther away, even my voice is getting farther away, and as it gets farther and farther away you are sinking down deeper, and deeper to

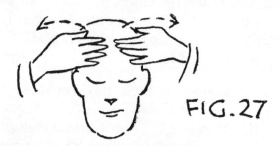

FIG. 27

Lower your voice and speak softer and softer as you give these suggestions about your voice getting farther away. Then gradually resume your normal tone. "You are going down deep asleep. Sleepy sleep. Sound, sound, asleep. Sleep deep! Your muscles are all relaxed. Your head is getting heavy, it is falling forward on your chest."

Gently give his head a little push so that it will fall

forward. Then begin stroking the back of his neck from the top back part of his head down to the base of his brain. In this stroking process locate the small depressed spot between the first and second vertebrae at the very top of the spinal column. Press in firmly upon this spot with the side of your right forefinger (See Fig. 28). It produces a deadening sensation as you suggest.

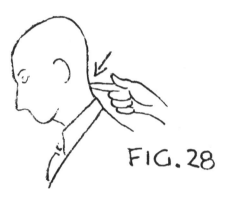

FIG. 28

"How numb everything feels. You are so drowsy and sleepy. Go sound asleep. Every muscle all over your body, from the very top of your head down to your very feet, is relaxed and restful."

Now place your hands in the center of his shoulders and press downward (See Fig. 29). Slump his body down in his chair as much as possible, and suggest, "Your hands and arms are so heavy. So very, very heavy. You can feel them weighing heavily in your lap. And the fingers are beginning to tingle. And your legs, too, are getting so heavy. They are pressing heavier upon the floor, as you sink down deeper and deeper to sleep.

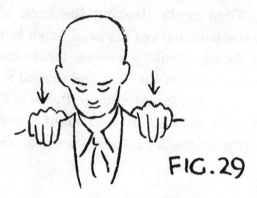

FIG. 29

"Now your breaths are beginning to deepen. Breathing deep and free. Breathe deep and free." **Place your head close to your subject's ear and inhale and exhale forcefully yourself. Watch the subject carefully at this point, and you will note that he picks up the tempo of your breathing as his inhalations become deep and full.** "Breathing deep and full. Deep and full. And every breath you take is sending you down deeper and deeper to sleep. Go sound asleep. Going sound, sound asleep—down deep, deep asleep."

Step now to the front of your subject and make long, slow downward passes from the top of his head to his lap. Make these in close to the body, but without contact (See Fig. 30).

Suggest, "Sound, sound sleep. See how limp and relaxed your arms are. They are limp just like rags." **Pick up one of his hands a trifle from his lap and let it drop back. Then push his hands deliberately from his lap, they will fall limply to his sides where they dangle rag-like.** "Nothing bothers you in the least. Just sleep quietly and calmly. My voice seems so very far, far away, but you are sleeping deep and peacefully.

"Now when I press your fingernails, you will pass on down deeper into an even more profound sleep—

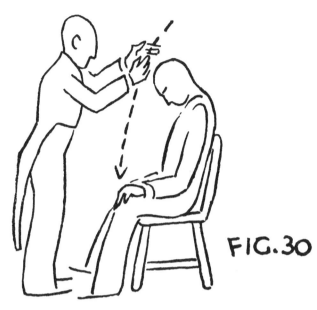

FIG. 30

way down deep into the very deepest of hypnotic sleeps." Pick up his hands, place them again upon his lap, and press with your thumbs upon the roots of the nails of his second and third fingers, between the first knuckle joint and the nail (See Fig. 31). Make the pressure firm and even as you suggest, "As I press on your

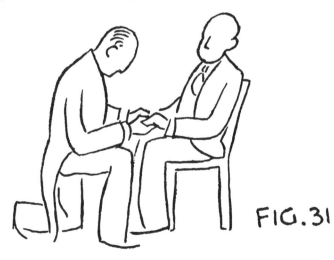

FIG. 31

fingers you are going deeper to sleep. Way down D - E - E - P ASLEEP! WAY DOWN DEEP A S L E E P!" **Pick up your subject's hands, hold them out free from his lap and let them suddenly drop. If they fall limply, directly to his sides, without resistance, dangling like rags; then suggest,** "Now as you sleep there, nothing will disturb you. You will follow every suggestion I present to you. Nothing will bother or disturb you in the least, and you will continue going on down deeper, and deeper to sleep."

You are now ready to experiment with the trance. Practice and master this method of hypnotizing well, for the progressive approach is very important to your later stage work.

It would be possible to present many additional techniques for inducing hypnosis, but since they are all basically the same, little would be gained. Here in this variety you have ample. As you proceed with your work you will soon develop your own style, techniques, and suggestion patters. It is exactly as in performing Magic, every Magician must work out his own presentation, routines, and the patter that best fits his particular personality.

The essential thing to keep in mind in the development of any hypnotic technique is that your method must capture and hold your subject's attention while you drive home suggestions that will be uncritically accepted. To such ends, conditions that will remove as much stimuli as is possible from the subject, and that will narrow and focus his attention field are necessary to maintain.

In fact, it is the deliberate control of these stimuli that is the means of our entering the state of mind we normally call "Sleep" night after night. Consider, at night we lie down, shut out the light—**the sense of** sight is nil, and that source of stimuli is removed. We lie quietly in bed—our sense of feeling and motion is restricted. The room is quiet and still—thus the auditory sense becomes lulled. In bed, also, the olfactory and taste senses are largely dormant. Thus comes SLEEP.

So it is in the induction of hypnosis—it is produced just like natural sleep, with the exception of one fundamental difference. In sleep all of the senses are dulled, while in hypnosis all of the senses are dulled with the exception of one. And that one is peaked. We know how it is in cases of blind, deaf, or dumb persons, when one or more of their senses are lost, the others tend to compensate and frequently develop to a hyper degree. In hypnosis, there is likewise this tendency ... and it is through the avenue of this heightened or peaked sense that a rapport to the mind of the subject is maintained, and suggestions may be implanted directly. The accompanying graphs show clearly the process.

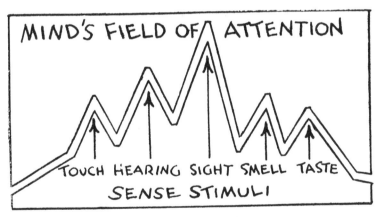

GRAPH A

In Graph A we have a person in his normal waking state. Note how a variety of stimuli are entering his "Mind's Field of Attention" in varying degrees of intensity. And Graph B shows the same person in the process of being hypnotized. Note how the variety of stimuli has been leveled out and one strongly emphasized.

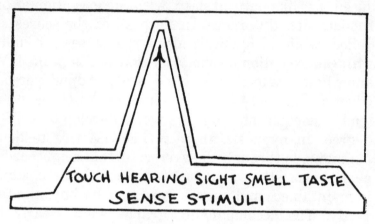

TOUCH HEARING SIGHT SMELL TASTE
SENSE STIMULI

GRAPH B

In actual practice the subject is seated comfortably relaxed back in a chair and told to move as little as is possible—thus the stimuli of Touch, Smell, and Taste are reduced to a minimum. The eyes are next fatigued and shortly closed; stimuli of sight is so removed. Only the sense of hearing remains, and it is through that heightened channel that suggestions are given to the mind. THUS COMES HYPNOSIS.

PHENOMENA OF THE TRANCE

Having hypnotized your subject — what has happened? There he sits relaxed back in the chair, head drooped forward, breathing heavily and looking very much as if he had merely dozed off into a little nap. Left to himself he would pass from the hypnotic condition, in which you have placed him, into perfectly normal sleep, and would awaken in anywhere from a few minutes to a few hours of his own accord.

However, at the moment, despite outward appearances, your subject is not asleep in the accepted sense of the term—he is hypnotized, and while in that state of mind is ready and willing to accept suggestions from you—which suggestions are capable of producing some most unusual and interesting phenomena characteristic of the hypnotic condition, i.e., muscular-catalepsy, somnambulistic-walking, illusions, hallucinations, and post-hypnotic effects. Let us try for each of these phenomena with a few experiments.

First, suggest to your hypnotized subject that his eyes are stuck tightly together, so tightly that he will be unable to open them no matter how hard he tries. Then ask him to try with all his might to open his eyes. He tries and tries, but in vain. The eyebrows rise and fall, but the eyelids remain stuck tightly shut. They simply refuse to open. Now tell him to relax his eyes, to forget about them, and to continue on sleeping deeply ... and proceed on to another muscular test.

But first remember this very important rule in the giving of hypnotic suggestions: **Having completed one series, before ever presenting a new set of suggestions**

to the hypnotized subject always remove your previous suggestions by telling him to forget what you have just said and to sleep on deeply. This is a vital point to keep in mind, otherwise one set of suggestions might conflict with the other.

Imagine what would happen if you told a subject he was unable to rise from his chair, and while he was trying in vain to do so, you suddenly suggested that he would feel an irrepressible impulse to rise at once. What happens? Well, in most cases the stronger of the two suggestions would dominate, and the subject would act accordingly. But, in the case of a very sensitive person, these two opposing suggestions, working simultaneously, might well develop a neurotic conflict which would be decidedly injurious to the subject, and lead to a bad case of hysteria. **So, in your experimenting make it a religious rule to give only one series of suggestions at a time, and always remove their effects from the subject before going on to another experiment.**

Take your subject's arm now and raise it out at a right angle to his body, suggesting that it is becoming stiff and rigid . . . rigid like a bar of steel. You will immediately feel the muscles in his arm tighten, and the arm will remain rigidly outstretched of its own accord. Now suggest that the arm is so stiff that he cannot move it—try as hard as he will. Your subject tries in vain to move his arm, but it resists all of his efforts. Now suggest that at the count of "Three" his arm will instantly relax, and will fall loosely to his side, and that the moment it hits his side, it will send him down deeper, ever deeper, to sleep. Count, "One two, three," and the arm suddenly goes limp and falls to his side.

You can fairly well judge by the way that arm falls just how deeply under the hypnotic influence your subject is. If the arm immediately collapses at your count of "Three," and falls limp like a rag to the subject's side, you can be more or less certain he is well in the trance. On the other hand, if he lowers his arm slowly, as though it's under tension and his own volition, it is a good indication that he is not as deeply affected as he should be, and that it would be well for you to continue your hypnotizing process longer before proceeding on to any further experiments.

In watching your subject's arm drop instantly from a cataleptic condition to complete relaxation, you are observing right here an example of the **extreme relaxation** hypnosis brings to the body, which is one of the valuable aspects of the hypnotic condition.

Now suggest to your subject that he will stand up from his chair, and that as he does so he will continue to sink down ever deeper to sleep. Command him to arise, and then to walk—and you will be observing a condition similar to the conventional "sleep walker." Indeed, you have induced hypnotic somnambulism. Next request the subject to return to his chair, to relax back in it, and to continue on going down deeper to sleep. You are now ready to experiment with an illusion.

An illusion, or false impression of an object, always requires a tangible article of some sort as the initial stimulus around which the illusion may form. In this case, for the center of the stimulus you hand the subject a broom and suggest that, in a moment, he will open his eyes and will see in his arms a beautiful girl. Then suggest that when you reach the count of "Three," he will open his eyes and look at this girl, that he will be very much in love with her, and will kiss her enthusiastically. Further suggest that when he opens his eyes and sees this girl it will send him down even further asleep in the hypnotic trance. Count, "One, two, three," and your subject will open his eyes, see the broom in his arms, definitely interpret it as being a beautiful girl with whom he is in love, and kiss it soundly.

This experiment illustrates not only a typical hypnotic illusion but likewise an example of the "foolish" type of hypnotic experiment. Such occasionally have their place in providing the lighter moments in the hypnotic entertainment, but you must be very careful in selecting the subjects you use for such. For while some persons would look upon such an exhibition as a lot of fun, others would be decidedly embarrassed by it . . . **and embarrassing your subjects is one thing you must never do.** After all, you are dealing with fellow human beings who have voluntarily placed themselves in your hands for the expressed purpose of conducting psychological experiments. This implies a confidence in you And as a Hypnotist you must ever respect that confidence. **By and large, make it your rule never to attempt any demonstration that you wouldn't be perfectly willing to have performed on yourself.**

Now suggest to your subject that his dream girl (the broom) is fading away, that his eyes are closing, and that he is going back to sleep. Gently take the broom away from him, and you are ready to try for an hallucination.

An hallucination is similar to an illusion in that it conjures up an imaginary impression (or sensation), but in the production of such it makes use of no material cue for the development of the illusion. In other words, an hallucination develops purely on the strength of your suggestions alone.

Tell your subject that he is now sleeping deeply, but that when you again count to "Three" he will open his eyes, will look at his left hand, and will see in it the cutest little canary bird he ever saw. Tell him that he will love this little bird, will play with it, and watch it fly all about the room. Now suggest again, that when you reach the count of "Three" he will open his eyes and look at this little bird in his left hand. Then count, "One, two, three." The subject opens his eyes, stares at his left hand, and goes through all the responses of playing with the little bird.

Does he actually see the canary? Yes, indeed, he does. To him that little bird is very, very real . . . a good hypnotic subject definitely believes that he is holding a bird and actually sees and feels that suggested bird. The resulting pantomime is truly amazing to behold. Finally, when the experiment has proceeded long enough, suggest that the bird is fading away and disappearing, and that he is getting sleepy again, that his eyes are closing, and that he is fast, fast asleep. From this test you can go directly into a post-hypnotic demonstration.

Suggest to your subject that in a moment you are going to awaken him, and that when he awakes he will feel fine and perfectly normal in all respects, except that he will find that he is stuck to his chair's seat, and is entirely unable to rise no matter how hard he tries. Repeat these suggestions again—that after he awakes he will feel fine, but that he will be stuck tightly to his seat, and try as he will he cannot rise up until you snap your fingers by his ear and tell him he can.

Now carefully awaken your subject by the method

to be described in the chapter, "Awakening the Subject," and casually ask him to get up from his chair. He will struggle and tug, very much surprised at his inability to rise; but try as he will, he is utterly unable to leave his seat; until you snap your fingers by his ear and say, "All right, you can get up now."

You can make an interesting observation here, if you like, by explaining to your subject, as he tries vainly to get up from his seat, that the only force that is holding him stuck to it are suggestions you presented to him while he was hypnotized. Sometimes that realization enables him to break the post-hypnotic effects, but often, even realizing such, he is utterly powerless to overcome the powerful effect of a suggestion set in his unconscious. You have thus experimentally produced a neurosis, and illustrated most beautifully how a complex works in our daily lives.

Post-hypnotic effects are among the most interesting in the entire field of Hypnotism. Many persons seem puzzled as to how a hypnotic suggestion can continue on after the condition of hypnosis is removed. However, when we regard Hypnotism as a state of mind in which ideas can be powerfully sold directly to the unconscious, post-hypnotic phenomena become the expected occurrence—just as any idea thoroughly learned becomes a continued part of our lives long after the original teacher is gone.

In this chapter you have been taken rapidly through a series of experiments which serve excellently to graphically illustrate some of more observable phenomena that may be produced in the hypnotic trance.

In experimenting with your subject, it is unlikely that you will wish to conduct all of these demonstrations at one sitting. Indeed, unless you have an exceptionally good subject it would hardly be possible to obtain all of these effects. However, these experiments, as outlined, have been built up step by step proceeding from the least difficult to the hardest. You see, many subjects are able to get muscular-catalepsy who are utterly unable to experience an hallucination, while some may experience an hallucination and yet not be able to feel post-hypnotic effects. So in experimenting, follow the approximate order of these tests, working up through catalepsy, illusions, hallucinations, to post-hypnotic phenomena. And when you obtain good post-hypnotic reactions, you may be sure that your subject has developed the capacity of entering the hypnotic trance to a very deep degree.

Of last consideration on the phenomena of the trance arises the question—does a subject remember what occurs to him after he awakens from the hypnotic sleep? Sometimes YES and sometimes NO. Hypnotic effects can be very real and very pronounced, and still the subject may retain a memory of them. Sometimes that memory is complete, and sometimes it is very hazy and vanishes quickly like a dream upon awakening. **But, when the trance is in its very deepest stages there is invariably amnesia—a decided lapse of memory.**

Let us now detail some of the many interesting experiments that you can perform.

EXPERIMENTS IN THE HYPNOTIC STATE

Now that you have learned how to Hypnotize, and have practiced producing some of the fundamental effects of hypnosis, there is an infinite variety of interesting experiments that you can try. **In the giving of your suggestions to the hypnotized subject to affect these experiments, your approach should now be one of command rather than request.** In other words, you tell your subject what he is to do . . . and the field and focus of his attention being so limited, the command is instantly picked up, obeyed, and interpreted.

As an example, in stiffening the arm you **do not** say, "Please hold up your arm. Now think of it becoming stiff. You can feel it getting rigid and tense," as you would in pre-hypnotic tests. Instead, you say very forcefully, "Raise your arm out straight. Your arm is stiff and rigid. You cannot bend it. Try hard to bend your arm. You cannot!" **Make all of your suggestions thus directly to the point so as to be easily understood by the subject, and tell him exactly what he is to do.**

For instance, the fishing scene: Let us suppose that you wish to make your subject think that he sees a lake in front of him. Tell him simply **exactly** what you want him to see before you have him open his eyes. Say to him thus, "When you open your eyes, you will see before you a beautiful blue lake. You will enjoy seeing this lake very much. All right, sit up in your chair and get ready to see this lake. I will count three, you will open your eyes, and will see clearly before you this beautiful blue lake. And as you watch this lake, it will send you continually down deeper and deeper asleep in the hypnotic trance." **There are some impor-**

tant bits of technique here in the setting of the hallucination to occur on a given cue, in this case, the opening of the eyes, and in the suggesting that witnessing the hallucination will deepen the sleep; otherwise, the surprise of seeing the hallucination might jerk the subject out of the trance.

Then count "One, two, three," the subject opens his eyes and goes through all of the pantomime of observing a beautiful lake (See Fig. 32).

FIG. 32

You can now lead your subject through various aspects of the scene by handing him a stick, telling him it is a fishing pole and that he is going fishing in the lake. If he is a person with an active imagination such will be sufficient, and he will portray the whole scene entirely on his own; baiting the hook, throwing the line in the lake, reeling in the fish, taking it off of the hook, etc.

But if he is lethargic, then you must induce the

various effects by simple commands of, "Bait your hook. Now throw your line in the lake and fish. That's it, you've got a bite now. Hook that fish. Reel him in, etc." The exact way you handle your subject obviously depends upon the mental make-up of the subject himself, but whatever your procedure to secure active responses, the resulting pantomimes are so true to life that you will be amazed at the results.

Having completed the test, tell him to close his eyes, to go back to sleep, that his fishing trip is now all over, and that all he has to do is simply sleep. The effects of the experiment are thus completely removed from his mind, and you are then ready to try for another test.

You can show him roses where none exist, you can make him think he is an orator or a singer, by a simple suggestion. After a subject has been deeply hypnotized it is not necessary to again put him to sleep to produce these illusions. Often if the effects are somewhat related, one to the other, the subject can be made to pass directly from each to the next. Always, however, tell him to go to sleep and that the illusion is all gone before conducting a new type of experiment of a conflicting nature.

Variety of Hypnotic Experiments

(Here is a splendid resume of various hypnotic experiments with proper acknowledgment to the studies of Dr. Bernard Hollander.)

In response to your direct and specific suggestions, your subject may be rendered happy and gay, or sad and dejected, angry or pleased, liberal or stingy, proud or humble, pugnacious or pacific, bold or timid, hopeful or despondent, insolent or respectful. He may be made to sing, to shout, to laugh, to weep, to act, to dance, to shoot, to fish, to preach, to pray, to recite a beautiful poem, or to excogitate a profound argument.

The expression of your subject during these delusions is most important as its very earnestness is profound in its appeal. The attitudes and gestures are equal to, or surpassing, the best efforts of the most accomplished actor, although the hypnotized subject may actually be a person of limited intellectual cultivation, and show no peculiar talent for mimicry in the waking state.

The hypnotized subject is not acting a part in the ordinary sense of the word. He believes himself to be the actual personality suggested. The subject will impersonate to perfection any suggested character with which he is familiar. Most effective tests can be performed by thus suggesting to your subject that he is some popular movie star such as Bing Crosby or Boris Karloff.

One of the most striking and important peculiarities of the unconscious mind, as distinguished from the conscious, consists in its prodigious memory. In all degrees of the hypnotic sleep, this exaltation of the memory is one of the most pronounced of the attendant phenomena.

One of the remarkable effects of hypnotism is this recollection of circumstances and the revival of impression long since past, the images of which have been completely lost to ordinary memory, and which are not recoverable in the normal state of mind. All the sensations which we have ever experienced have left behind them traces in the brain, so slight as to be intangible and imperceptible under ordinary circumstances; but hypnotic suggestion, addressing itself to the unconscious side of the mind, and the unconscious mind being the storehouse of memories, can be recalled at the command of the operator. Fascinating experiments can be tried in having the subject recall and relive episodes way back in his past, such as suggesting, "You're now way back in the third year of your life. You are attending your third year birthday party; tell us what happened."

Everything learned in normal life can be remembered in hypnosis, even when apparently it has long been forgotten.

Of course, false-memories can also be suggested, as when you say to a subject, "Of course, you remember we drove to Richmond, yesterday," and if it is at all plausible that we may have done so, the suggestion will take effect, and he will at once begin to relate all that he believes we did in Richmond. This is an example of a retro-active positive hallucination, because the subject believes that he has experienced something that really never occurred. This not only happens in the hypnotic state, but in the waking state in some people, especially children with a lively imagination.

Memory may also be obliterated. Nothing is easier than to make the subject forget his name and condition in life. This is one of the suggestions which most promptly succeed, even with a very new subject. The subject may forget whole periods of his life at the suggestion of the hypnotizer.

Sense delusions are likewise common in Hypnotism; either as hallucinations or illusions. An illusion, you will recall, is the false interpretation of an existing external object, as, for instance, when a chair is taken for a lion, a broomstick for a beautiful woman, a noise in the street for orchestra music, or when you ask a subject whether he would like to smoke, and he accepts a lead pencil in place of a cigarette and attempts to light it. That the illusion is real is evident by the fact that the subject will imagine he is drawing smoke from the pencil, which, of course, is not even alight, and will even cough, if smoking is usually irritating to his throat.

Try these experiments with illusions: Play on a real piano. Then suggest that a table is a piano, and play on that. Ask your subject which piano he likes the best, and he will take the real one. Give your subject an empty glass and tell him it contains hot whiskey and water, and that he must take care not to burn his mouth. The ensuing endeavor to swallow the imaginary liquor is followed by catching of the breath and violent coughing.

As we have already discussed, an hallucination is the perception of an object which does not exist, as for instance, when you say to your subject, "Sit down in this armchair," where there is really no chair at all; yet the hallucination is so perfect that he does put himself in exactly the same attitude as if he were sitting in a real chair, only if you ask him after a time, "Are you comfortable?" he may reply, "Not particularly," and ask for a chair that is more comfortable. It seems incredible that an hallucination could be so real that a person would assume an attitude so strained, but it is so.

Suggest to a person that a swarm of bees are buzzing about him; he will not only see and hear them, but he will go through violent antics to beat them off. Or tell a person that there are rats in the room, and the word will wake up a train of imagery in the subject's brain which is immediately projected outward in an expressive display of appropriate gestures of aversion and corresponding movements of avoidance.

The fear depicted on the face of a subject when he believes he is about to be attacked by a tiger is most impressive. **But, such suggestions—inspiring terror—should never be made.**

Hallucinations of all the senses and delusions of every conceivable kind can be easily suggested to a good subject. Just how real these effects are to the subject is evidenced in experiments where the image of the hallucination has been caused to double by a prism or mirror, magnified by a lens, and in many other ways behaves optically like a real object.

In suggesting an hallucination, say that of a bird, the suggested approach of the object causes contraction of the pupil, and vice versa. At the same time, there is often convergence of the axis of the eyes, as if a real object were present.

Subjects will eat a potato for a peach, or drink a cup of vinegar for a glass of champagne. He may be thrown into a state of intoxication by being caused to drink a glass of water under the impression that it is gin; or he may be restored to sobriety by the administration of gin under the guise of an antidote to drunkenness. In these cases the expression of the face induced by the suggested perception corresponds so perfectly that a better effect would scarcely be produced if the real article were used.

Various physiological effects can be produced in the state of hypnosis. A subject can be caused to weep and shed tears on one side of the face and laugh with the other. The pulse can be quickened or retarded, respiration slowed or accelerated, or temporarily arrested, and perspiration can be produced—all by suggestion. Even the temperature can be affected. Thus it has been observed that if a subject is told he has a high fever his pulse will become rapid, his face flushed, and his temperature increased. Or, if a person is told that he is standing on ice he feels cold at once. He trembles, his teeth chatter, he wraps himself up in his coat. "Gooseskin" can be produced by the suggestion of a cold bath. Hunger and thirst can be created, and other functions increased or retarded.

The mind can be so concentrated upon a physiological process as to stimulate that process to normal activity, so as to produce curative effects, and even to super-abundant activity, so as to produce pathological effects or disease. For instance, a blister can be caused on a sound and healthy skin by applying a postage stamp and suggesting that it is a strong mustard plaster; or placing upon the skin a key or coin, with the suggestion that after waking, a blister will appear at the spot where the key or coin had been placed, and of corresponding size and shape. The key or coin is then removed and the patient awakened, having no conscious knowledge of the suggestion given; but at the appointed time the blister appears.

On the other hand, blisters and burns have been annulled by suggestion. Mere local redness of the skin is easily produced by suggestion, and can be seen to appear in a few minutes by watching the subject.

Naturally, several organs can be influenced by suggestion at the same time. Tell someone, "Here is a rose." At once your subject not only sees, but feels and also smells the rose. The suggestion here affects sight, feeling and smell at the same time.

When the delusion is positive, the hypnotic believes he sees what does not exist; when it is negative, he fails to recognize the presence of an object really placed before him. An excellent experiment is to suggest to the subject, that on awaking he will not be able to see you, although you will remain in the room so he can feel and hear you, and although he will see everybody else. The subject on being awakened can hear and feel you, but he fails entirely to see you. When speaking to him you will observe his head and eyes turn in the direction of your voice, but you are completely invisible to him. This is a negative hallucination of sight. Similarly, it may be suggested that the subject is deaf to certain words, but not to others.

An entire cessation of the functions of any sense organ can be induced in the same way as a negative hallucination. The sense organ affected is insusceptible of anything. A command suffices to restore the functions. It is certain that the blindness and deafness induced this way are of a mental nature, for the corresponding organ of sense performs its function, though the impressions do not reach the consciousness. In the same way, the sight of one eye can be suspended, though the other can see as usual. Try the experiment of suggesting to the hypnotized subject that he is totally blind and observe the baffling effect; do not prolong this test overly long, however.

The production of reddening and bleeding of the skin in hypnotized subjects suggested by tracing lines or pressing objects thereupon, puts (in a new light) the accounts handed down to us of the stigmata of the cross appearing on the hands, feet, sides and forehead of certain mystics. It is doubtful that the Magician will have much occasion to make use of these physiological effects of which the trance is capable, but they do serve to show its power.

Post-Hypnotic Suggestion

The sense of time appears to be an innate mental power, for there have been cases of idiot boys who were able to guess the time correctly, no matter how suddenly the question was put to them. Post-hypnotic suggestions make use of this time-sense being deferred suggestions given to the subject during hypnosis . . . and the suggestions may be given to occur at a specified time.

It appears wonderful to most people that an event should take place at whatever time may have been suggested to the subject while in the trance, whether in one, two, or twenty-four hours, or 1,000 or 2,000 minutes, or in a month or more remote periods from the day on which a subject has been hypnotized. Bramwell has performed many successful experiments this way, as, for example, the following; A woman was told that in so many thousand minutes she is to write her name, the hour of the day, and the date. She was not very well educated and, therefore, was not likely to work out the number of hours and minutes successfully, and yet, at the time appointed, she wrote down her name and put the date and hour, and was surprised to find what she had done. In another case, he told a young lady, aged nineteen, to make the sign of the cross after the lapse of 4,335 minutes. In spite of the fact that she had forgotten all about the suggestion, she fulfilled it accurately.

When the mind is made up to perform a certain action at a certain time, the idea is then dismissed from the mind; but if the unconscious has been properly trained, at the definite time, or reasonably near it, the action will be performed, although neither the thought of the time nor the idea of performing the action may have been in the mind from the moment that the resolution was taken and was put on one side to make room for other ideas. Here in these time experiments with post-hypnotic suggestion, the creative Magician has some phenomena that really savors of Magic.

Sometimes no definite time is given, but it is suggested that at a time marked by a signal, a certain event is to take place. The moment the signal occurs, the subject, who until then seems in a perfectly normal waking condition, will experience the effect of the suggested event. The conducting of such experiments are simple; as for example: suggest to your hypnotized subject, "When you awaken you will feel perfectly normal in every way, but when I touch the lobe of my ear you will experience an irresistable impulse to leave your chair, walk to the center of the room and stretch yourself. You will have no memory whatsoever of this command when you awaken, but the moment I touch the lobe of my ear you will immediately leave your chair, go to the center of the room and stretch yourself." Awaken your subject, and shortly touch the lobe of your ear and watch what happens—he will respond exactly as you instructed him in the trance, yet in his present state he will have no recollection at all of these instructions. When questioned why he did tne act, he will probably pass it off with a shrug, or rationalize about it—that he just felt like stretching. Actually, the post-hypnotic impulse is so powerful that the subject was unable to resist the tug of it the moment your "cue" set off the response.

In the same manner, you can re-hypnotize your subject by the post-hypnotic command that when you give a certain signal that he will instantly return again to the hypnotic sleep. This is a very important test for stage use as a demonstration of "Instantaneous Hypnotism." Tell your subject that when you point your finger at him, no matter what he is doing, that he will go instantly deep asleep. In the course of some later experiments, suddenly so point your finger, and witness the amazing reaction.

Another test of this same order is to hypnotize a number of subjects, and give them all the post-hypnotic suggestion that when you drop a handkerchief they will immediately go sound asleep and instantly collapse. Awaken your subjects, stand them in a row on the stage. Then drop the handkerchief. They fall like dead men to the stage, relaxed bundles of sleeping humanity.

Of course, post-hypnotic suggestions that excite ridicule should be avoided, even on subjects who volunteer for the experiment, and it must be make a consciencious rule that subjects are never to be used for such purposes.

Through post-hypnotic suggestions you can prevent another hypnotist from influencing your subject, in fact, you can even suggest a resisting power against your own influence. Conversely, you can increase that influence.

States of mind can be influenced, the subject made happy, sad, etc. Hunger and thirst or loss of appetite can be induced, personal character may be influenced. In general, with a good subject, all of the effects that can be produced in the trance can be likewise produced in the post-hypnotic state.

Extraordinary Phenomena of Hypnotism

Let us take up first such phenomena of the unconscious state as the hyper-aesthesia of the senses and the accentuation of the innate mental qualities and tendencies.

Taking a normal subject in the hypnotic state and blindfolding him, one of the first observations that can be made, refers to the probable existence of a "human aura;" for by holding one or more fingers near any part of the subject's body or head, without coming in actual contact, that part will be moved in the direction in which the finger is slowly drawn. An ordinary horseshoe magnet, held similarly, produces a like result. Subjects have been found so sensitive to this influence of the magnet, that even though they were unaware that such an instrument was in the room, complained of unpleasant sensations, when the magnet was held near the back of their head.

Bramwell says on this point, "The enigmatic reports of the effect of magnets, even if they be due, as many contend, to unintentional suggestion on the operator's part, certainly involve hyper-aesthetic perception; for the operator seeks as well as possible to conceal the moment when the magnet is brought into play, and yet the subject not only finds it out that moment in a way difficult to understand, but may develop effects which (in the first instance certainly) the operator did not expect to find."

Magnets seem to give off effects very similar to that produced when passes are made with the hands. Here may be one of the reasons why passes are so valuable to use in your hypnotic technique. **Many subjects can feel very plainly a tingling sensation as the hands pass over their body.**

Hollander writes on this point, "There is no doubt, in my mind, that a magnet gives off some force which can be felt by a hypnotized subject, and that our own body, particularly at the fingers' ends, exerts a similar influence. I became convinced of this by placing a hypnotized subject in a completely darkened room, then letting him open his eyes and describe what he saw. I held a magnet suspended in my hand at the poles of which he perceived a luminous appearance, and when holding out my fingers, he described similar luminous emanations proceeding from my fingertips.

"The magnetic, or odylic influence is characterized, like heat, light, and electricity, as being sent forth in all directions, and by its emanations being luminous to sensitive persons, in the dark. The light is very feeble, so as generally to be overpowered by the faintest glimmer of ordinary light; although very sensitive persons, and most persons when in the hypnotic sleep, can see it in daylight. I would here, in recommending the repetition and prosecution of these attractive researches by enquirers, urge on them the absolute necessity of following the conditions laid down.

"In order to see the odylic light, for example, not only must the subject be sensitive, but the darkness must be absolute, and if not at once successful, the sensitive should remain in darkness for an hour. Not the smallest gleam of light, even if the dullest daylight or a candle, must be allowed to enter at a chink, cranny, door, or window. None of the audience should go out or come in during the experiment; for if the door be opened, the admission, for an instant of light from the next room may spoil the performance.

"It is not unlikely that the human organism is a radio-active body, for if our experiments do not deceive us, the body emits rays which can be seen and felt by sensitive persons. There appears to be a "human aura" which extends from the body for a distance,—some say a yard—and gradually fades away. And the aura of each person is seen to be colored according to the vibrations belonging to his prevailing mental states or character. That these rays can be seen I have already shown. The following is an experiment which I have often repeated, which would prove that they can also be felt. A hypnotized and blindfolded subject is made to distinguish a person's hand from a dozen others, when held above his or hers at a distance of six inches or less for a few seconds. This can be done with great success, and if you give numbers to the different persons present, the subject will, after a time, even recognize when the hand of No. 5 or 7 or any other, comes around again."

In experimenting with any of these mysterious forces, which are admitted, by those who believe in their existence, to be very feeble in power, your suggestions must be handled very carefully, for suggestion is stronger than any magnetic force, and, unless guarded against, can falsify your results.

Other super-normal effects can be found in the increasing to hyper-states the subject's ability to see and hear. Blindfold your subject and suggest that he can now see through the bandage. In many cases, he will be able to read a book under such normally impossible conditions. Hearing can likewise be increased by suggesting that he can hear very clearly and distinctly, and then taking a position well out of his normal hearing range and giving a whispered command which will be followed.

Here is a fascinating experiment in these super-sensitized hypnotic abilities. Take a deck of cards.

Have a card selected, and its name noted. Then hand it to your subject back upward, and tell him that it is a picture of his mother, that he will be able to recognize and locate that picture under any conditions and at any time. Then mix the card up in the deck and hand the entire pack, back uppermost, to the subject. One by one he will run through the cards, until finally stopping at one card which he will declare is the photo of his mother. On turning the card over, it will be found the one chosen.

The explanation of this surprising demonstration is that every playing card, no matter how new or seemingly unmarked, has on it some minute difference that sets it apart from its neighbors. In this experiment, in the course of the illusion of seeing his mother's picture, the subject interprets into the illusions these differences, through hyper-sensitized abilities, to such an extent that he is able to distinguish that card by its back from amongst all of the others; the observing of the particular, nearly invisible variations, again calling to the fore the suggested illusion.

Extra Sensory Perception in the Trance—Telepathy

Hypnotize your subject, suggest to him that he will feel an electric-like tingling sensation from your fingers as you pass them down his arm, and as he feels it, that his arm will slowly raise up from his lap.

Make the passes down his right arm from the elbow to the fingertips, and slowly the arm will raise. Then repeat the experiment making passes down his left arm until that hand, too, lifts up.

Now explain that you are not going to tell him over which hand you are making the passes, but that as he feels the tingling sensation he is to raise up that hand. Experiment thus a few times. Then suggest that he will feel the same sensations in his hands merely when you think of his raising up either of his hands, and that he is to lift up the hand in which he notes the tingles.

Then concentrate on his raising either his right or left hand as you desire. In transmitting a telepathic impulse, such as lifting of a hand, do not merely say over and over to yourself, "Lift your hand, lift your hand," **rather visualize in your mind an image of the subject actually lifting up the specific hand.**

Next have your subject stand up with his feet together, explaining that he will feel an impulse to take a step forwards or a step backwards, and that when he senses such, he is to step accordingly. Then flip a coin, if it comes up HEADS concentrate on him stepping forward; if it's TAILS, then backwards. **Always tabulate your results.**

Take two subjects, hypnotize them and suggest they are in rapport—that one is the transmitter and the other receiver. Touch the hand of the "transmitter" and tell him to concentrate on the other subject lifting the corresponding hand, the "receiver" understanding that he is to lift up the hand that he feels an impulse to raise.

Generally speaking, telepathic ideas of movements are the simplest to transmit, but you can also experiment with cards, numbers, colors, pictures, letters, and words. **Always make sure that your hypnotized subject understands exactly what test you propose to try and what is expected of him.**

Although it has not been experimentally proven to the satisfaction of science, many operators claim that they have successfully hypnotized susceptible subjects over a distance of many miles through the use of telepathy. Try the experiment first by placing the subject in another room from you, then later try the test over a distance of miles. In the process, close your eyes and get a clear image of the subject before you. Then repeat over and over to yourself mentally, "You must go sound asleep, you are so sleepy, you cannot stay awake, you will go sound asleep, you are now in a deep, deep sleep. Now you are asleep. You will follow my suggestions." Unless you can get a good, clear image of the subject before you, you are not likely to succeed. After closing your eyes, always wait until you get a strong visualization before you begin your mental suggestions.

Unless such experiments are carefully recorded they have little value. Arrange to check the time you started and finished the experiment, and have your subject do likewise.

Clairvoyance

Place your subject into the deepest possible hypnotic sleep, making use of the method next to be described. When he has passed into a deep trance, continue to make long sweeping passes over his entire body, starting at the head and ending at the feet (See Fig. 33).

After your subject is as deeply hypnotized as you feel it is possible to get him, take out your watch and hold it to his forehead, and tell him that you want him to tell you what time it is; that he can see the watch without any trouble; that he can see the time of day. Then ask him again if he can see what time it is. If he says he cannot, ask him what you can do to make him see plainer. If he tells you anything, **do as he tells you.**

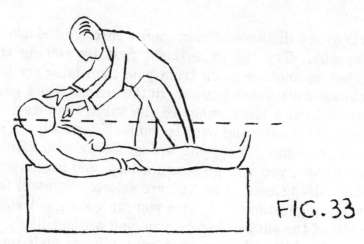

FIG. 33

If he does not tell you what to do, make some passes over his forehead quickly and ask him if he can now see plainer. If he says, "Yes," make a few more passes and insist that he tell the time. At this point you should be very emphatic. **Force him to see.** Should the test fail, you may write a single figure on a slip of paper, put it in an envelope and hold it to his head, and see if he can tell you what figure it is. Also ask him to describe to you some place where he has been. If he gives you a good, clear description, then ask him about some place which you have visited, but which he has not. Do not expect to succeed every time you try, for if you did, then there would be no question about the existence of these extra sensory powers. And remember, you must develop your subjects for such tests; try the process every day for a week or two on one subject before you pass judgment. Some can never be developed. In fact, it seems that comparatively few persons only are susceptible of entering this clairvoyant state; so you may have to try ten or fifteen subjects before you find one that is suitable. And when you do find a person who promises something in this direction do not use him in other tests—concentrate all of his hypnotic efforts in psychic directions, and the more you practice on such tests the better he will become.

Hypnotic Method for E.S.P. Experiments

Get a blue light and direct it so it shines over the forehead of your subject as he lies prone on a couch. Take your seat beside him, and have him gaze into your eyes (See Fig. 34).

FIG. 34

Then begin making passes towards his face gently, and very softly suggest that his eyes are getting heavy and are closing. When his eyes are closed, make passes over his face, telling him now to go to sleep, down deep into a trance.

In this method keep your verbal suggestions to an absolute minimum. Your whole approach must be just the opposite of forceful; being extremely gentle, almost ascetic. You are attempting to arouse phychic abilities, so concentrate on mental commands by visualizing your subject going to sleep, passing down, step by step, deeper and deeper into the trance.

Next stand up beside your subject, and leaning over him make the long passes, starting at his head and passing down the entire length of his body ending at the feet. In making these passes, extend your fingers outstretched and tense and imagine that you can feel a magnetic current passing out of them. Soon you will actually seem to feel a tingling sensation in your fingertips (See Fig. 35).

FIG. 35

Then place your extended fingers over your subject's forehead, and in short circular strokes endeavor to transmit the "force" (See Fig. 36).

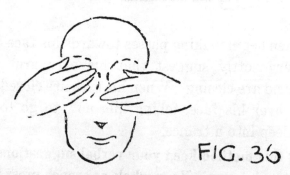

FIG. 36

As you make these passes, concentrate continuously on your mental suggestions of the subject going to sleep down deep into the trance. Keep your attention rapt and intent. Then bring your hands on slowly down his body in straight passes, stopping at the heart, and making further short circle-like passes. Make these passes without contact, about six inches above the body, and continue on down to the very feet. When you reach the feet, violently give your hands a flip as though you were throwing off from the fingers an imaginary sticky substance, turn your hands palm outward and again approach your subject's head . . . turn your hands palm inward over his forehead, and repeat the process of long passes over the full-length of his outstretched body.

Continue these passes for about ten minutes, and when you feel your subject is deeply entranced, proceed testing for Extra Sensory Powers.

Needless to say, these experiments of psychical nature are too erratic and uncertain in their results to warrant their use on the stage by the Magician, but they are splendid for parlor entertaining. Nothing fascinates an intimate group more than to experiment thus with the mysterious forces of the mind.

AWAKENING THE SUBJECT

The one phase of Hypnotism that the general public seems to worry the most about is the removing of the trance. In fact, there are circulated far too many wild stories of how persons have been hypnotized, and then the operator was unable to bring them back to consciousness, and a physician had to be called in to awaken them. Now, actually you need never experience the slightest difficulty in awakening the subject.

Since hypnosis is induced by a process of suggestion affirming ideas of going to sleep, it stands to reason that the reverse of that process—presenting suggestions for the removal of that sleep and awakening from the trance are bound to remove the hypnotic condition. Hence, the only possible reason for any difficulty, whatsoever, in awakening the subject must lie in faulty technique, applied by some operators.

How many, many times I have watched a hypnotist make use of a slow, methodical method in inducing the hypnotic trance, and then, when ready to awaken the person, suddenly clap his hands like a bolt of thunder directly in his subject's ear, and shout a loud, "WAKE UP!" I've seen such subjects literally leap out of their seats under the impulse of that command. Is it any wonder that with such violent methods a fear of the removal of hypnosis has developed?

After all, the hypnotizing process produces a shift in consciousness just as sleep is a shift in consciousness . . . and how would you feel if someone so violently woke you up suddenly from a good, sound slumber? So it is in awakening from hypnosis, **the shift in the fields of consciousness must always be a gradual one—**

never a sudden shock.

If you will just keep in mind that in inducing the hypnotic condition, you presented your suggestions slowly and with care, and apply this same gentle and calm approach to the removal of the trance . . . you will never have the slightest difficulty. And remember, **as a hypnotist it is your moral obligation to always awaken your subject feeling better than he did when you started to hypnotize him.** To that end, follow these directions in detail for the removal of the hypnotic trance:

Having caused all the suggestions of your hypnotic experiments to fade away from the mind of your subject, and suggested that he is sleeping calmly and peacefully—present these suggestions.

"In a moment I am going to awaken you, and when you wake up you will feel just fine, relaxed, and refreshed — just good all over. Now, I am going to count very slowly from one to five, and with every count you will awaken more and more until by the time I reach five you will be wide awake. And when you wake up, say, you're going to feel so good. You've had the best sleep and rest you've ever experienced, and you're going to awaken in a few seconds now just full of vim, vitality, and pep—just feeling swell! All right now, I'm going to count from one to five . . . remember, with every count you will slowly, gently, and gradually awaken—and when I reach five be wide awake. All right, I'm starting to count—so get ready to wake up. **One, Two** . . .. you are beginning to awaken now; beginning to wake up. **Three** . . . your eyes are opening; you want to move about and stretch. **Four** . . . waking up. And **Five!** Wake up . . . wide awake . . . that's it, wide, wide awake. Awake and feeling fine."

Under the influence of these suggestions, your

subject will gradually open his eyes, move about, stretch himself, and will awaken **just feeling fine.**

Note how gradual that process of removing the hypnotic trance has been. How gentle and considerate it is; how the subject is set for the awakening before it even begins—he expects it, and when it does start, how it develops step by step. Notice, likewise, how suggestions are constantly repeated to the effect that when the subject awakens he will feel fine and good all over. **If you will apply this technique conscientiously, your subject will always awaken from his hypnotic sleep feeling refreshed and splendid . . . and will have enjoyed his hypnotic experience immensely.**

In concluding this chapter on "Awakening the Subject," let us point out a basic fact of Hypnotism— **there is never any danger of the subject not awaking from the trance . . . left entirely to himself the subject will speedily pass from the hypnotic sleep into natural sleep, and will awaken of his own accord precisely as he does on arising each morning.**

A BIT OF THEORY

With all of this care being spent to master the art of hypnotizing, it is only natural for the Magician to ask the question, WHAT IS HYPNOTISM? . . . if for no other reason than to arrange his "patter" intelligently in addressing his subjects and his audience.

Collin Bennett writes, "The practice of hypnotism is as straight-forward as its theory is involved. A good hypnotic subject can be got under the influence almost as quickly as you can snap a switch to turn on the electric light. In each instance there is the effect, but just what has brought it about? What is electricity? What is hypnotism?"

Well, what is Hypnotism?

For an answer to that question, let us consider the power any idea **in which we believe** holds upon our lives. After all, the sum total of our beings are the thoughts we think—for our thoughts lead directly to our actions and daily activities . . . and those thoughts which make up the very especial personality which is US are the deep rooted ideas which have been constantly hammered by environment, education, and experience into our minds. The word **hammered** is used, for it is the right word—for ideas hammered in either by great force, repetition, or emotional drive are the very ideas that stick with us, and are the ideas that become a part of our personalities and form the basis for our habits, fears, and complexes. **Such ideas so set in our nervous systems produce unconscious responses.** In other words, we have so learned these ideas that we no longer have to deliberately think about them; rather, their action has become automatic. Such ideas, to use a psychological term, have become **conditioned** into the nervous patterns of our lives as it were. Or, in a sense, we might say, that such ideas have been actually **hypnotized** into our minds.

For hypnotism is that uncritical state of mind in which ideas will be largely accepted without qualification, and in which our nervous systems may be conditioned most rapidly.

For example: Suppose you should hypnotize a man and tell him that when he awakens he will stutter and be entirely unable to speak clearly. What happens when he wakes up? He stutters!

Now, while he is wondering about this unexpected disturbance in his speech, you assure him that it is only your suggestions (or ideas), presented to him while he was hypnotized, that are making him stutter, and that surely he can overcome such an influence. Occasionally, with such an understanding of the cause of his condition being thus made clear to him, the man can throw off the influence and again speak clearly. But, if he has been deeply affected, he cannot do so even when so rationalizing about his problem. For, you see, the idea of his difficulty of speech has been so set in his nervous system that it is no longer under his voluntary control—it has become an unconscious response, a habit. **Through hypnosis he has been conditioned to stuttering, and a temporary oral neurosis has been developed.**

Now, let us consider stuttering in the case of a man in his perfectly normal state of mind. This man stutters. We reason with him that there is nothing basically wrong with his vocal cords, that his stuttering is purely a mental condition; surely he can master it. He still stutters. We ask him to try harder. He does, and, indeed, it seems that the harder he tries the worse he stutters. Why? Because the idea of stuttering is so set as a habit in his mind that he no longer has voluntary control over it.

Is there any especial difference between our hypnotically induced stutter and this one? Basically there is none. The one was **sold** the idea of stuttering rapidly and quickly while under hypnosis, while the other was **sold** the idea of such behavior as a result of a long series of activities developed through the course of his life. Since hypnotism can thus sell to the nervous system so efficiently ideas directly comparable to those developed in the process of years of normal living; it is self-evident the great power that is Hypnotism's.

Through this observation you will note that Hypnotism is obviously not some isolated mystic phenomenon, but is rather an induced state of mind with direct parallels to the normal development of our behavior patterns.

But what is hypnosis itself? Is it sleep? Frankly it is not, although to outward appearances it does very closely resemble such; and in its induction repeated ideas of sleep are given, and sleep-like conditions are closely simulated. But there is one great basic difference between sleep and hypnosis. In sleep, the attention of the sleeper is diffused, and the rapport (avenue of communication to the mind) is en-rapport—directed within himself. While in hypnosis, the attention is greatly peaked, and there is a direct and very keen rapport between the hypnotist and the hypnotized.

Hypnotism thus might be defined, **as a deliberately induced state of mind in which the subject is extremely** acute; the focus of his awareness being entirely centered only on the direct ideas presented to his mind by the hypnotist. And so sharply focused is this attention on the part of the subject, that when the trance is ended a condition of amnesia often results.

Following this "bit of theory" of Hypnotism being regarded as a state of mind producing a condition of hyper-attention, its ability to impress ideas (to condition) rapidly and powerfully upon the nervous system becomes evident. We all know that in the process of learning the greater the degree of attention we focus on the subject to be learned, the greater the impression it makes upon us; and the more rapidly and thoroughly we learn it. In the hypnotic trance, therefore, having the very height in attention, we reach the pinnacle of the mind's ability to rapidly learn.

QUESTIONS AND ANSWERS

In this chapter, let us round out our hypnotic knowledge and consider some questions which, as a Hypnotist, you will frequently be called upon to answer; and let us study suggestions which will make you a better operator. First on our list comes:

What percentage of persons can be hypnotized?

Every human being who is mentally sound can be influenced; some speedily and others with repeated trials. But the degree of that influence varies with different persons. Some are capable of deep somnambulistic phenomena — even including post-hypnotic, while others will only respond as far as muscular-catalepsy tests.

Taking an average of all humanity, roughly speaking, one person in five may be classed as being **a natural somnambulist** who has the ability to enter the hypnotic state, to its deepest extent, on the very first trial. However, that percentage can be greatly increased by working with a subject in a series of repeated attempts, over a period of time. For being hypnotized is very much like developing proficiency in any skill, some individuals seem to have a natural talent for entering the state, while others have to learn the hard way of repeated effort. And as always, in the cultivation of any ability—"practice makes perfect."

Is hypnotism inclined to weaken the will?

That question is a hangover from the old superstitious days produced by the Svengali type of hypnotist who **seemed** to completely dominate and master the mind of his subject, upon the stage, as though he were a weak-willed puppet. Actually, even in the case of such a performer, the domination was more an illusion than a fact; for **Will** has very little to do with the trance, and it can be definitely stated that Hypnotism does not weaken the Will. Indeed, it is possible through hypnosis to strengthen and develop those traits of character usually associated with Will-power, namely: increased determination of purpose, better concentration, more forceful individuality, and self-confidence.

Directly associated with this question is this:

Is a weak-willed person easier to hypnotize than a strong-minded individual?

Decidedly not! Those very factors that go into the making of a determined, forceful personality are the ones most needed for the successful induction of hypnosis. Generally speaking, weak-willed persons are those incapable of seriously holding thoughts in their minds sufficiently for the successful pursuance of any idea, and, as such, form the worse possible hypnotic subjects.

The above comment is not meant to infer that super-intelligence is an indispensable factor, helpful as it frequently is, in the induction of hypnosis. Rather than intelligence, reference is being made to the personality factor of the **emotional drive** to pursue to its completion a given objective.

Can a person be hypnotized against his will?

No, except in cases of "fear hypnosis." The entire process upon which Hypnotism is based is on the "ideo-motor theory," that an idea must be held in the mind's field of attention in order to produce hypnosis ... and, to be so deliberately centered, it is obvious that the idea must possess all absorbing interest. If ever you observe a person hypnotized, you may be sure the state was induced by his own motivation. Occasionally, a person may seem to be influenced almost automatically, so that it appears as if he did not give his willing consent to being hypnotized. But in such a case, the answer lies in the fact that consent to entering the hypnotic condition can be an **unconscious motivation** as well as a deliberate one. These latter cases, however, are the exception, not the rule, so, for all practical purposes, it can be made a general statement that the subject must be willing to be hypnotized before he can enter the state.

Another question in this regard; one that we have already considered at some length.

Is it possible to scare a person into hypnosis?

Yes, in some cases. For instance, we all know how if we **fear** that we are going to make a social blunder while attending an important banquet, we almost invariably make that blunder. That principle is the working of the Power of Suggestion—the **expectation** set in the mind of the person, leading directly to an automatic performance of the act, even though the Will does not sanction the action. Here is a case of the unconscious acceptance of an idea producing the effect rather than the consciousness of the person deliberately willing the act. This principle we discussed as a basic law of suggestion—**When the Imagination and the Will are in conflict, the Imagination invariably wins.**

As to scaring a person into hypnosis . . . from the above observation it is obvious that if the subject has a powerful **fear** that he is going to be hypnotized, it requires but little Svengali dramatics, on the part of the hypnotist, to **set off** this unconscious response, and literally scare his subject into the trance.

Sydney Flower cites an example of how stage operators can occasionally make use of this principle to produce a demonstration of **Instantaneous Hypnosis.** He writes, "The fact is that fear creates a bewilderment in the brain of the subject in which it is possible to suddenly drive home a positive suggestion with such force that it is permanently established. Occasionally there comes upon the stage, in response to a call for further volunteers after your first demonstration is complete, a person who, goaded on by the laughter of his companions, asserts that he is not afraid to be hypnotized; but the memory of what he has just witnessed, and his own natural fear of some 'force' which he does not understand, combine to make him a prey to the liveliest apprehensions, and though he shows a bold front, he is really very much unnerved. Pride, however, will not allow him to withdraw, and the result is that he puts up the best front he can muster and mounts to the stage. The Hypnotist, by reason of his experience, can instantly detect such signs of fear in the countenance of his voluntary subject, and he reads this man at a glance. He knows that if he can catch him quickly and drive in his suggestion he will have no trouble in putting this party instantly asleep. But quick suggestion alone is not sufficient to to induce the instant bewilderment of the senses which is required to produce such sudden hypnosis.

"Therefore, the Hypnotist steps forward to the edge of the platform, and as the subject gets one foot upon the stage, the professor suddenly claps one hand on the back of the subject's neck, which appears to the audience to be merely an eager method of helping the subject on the stage. It really has the effect of still further bewildering the subject, and without giving the latter further time, the hypnotist brings the palm

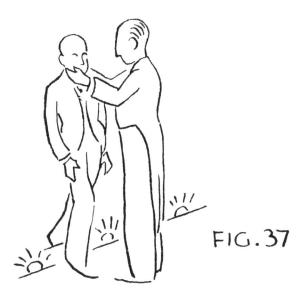

FIG. 37

of his other hand with some force against the chin of the subject, thus producing a sudden nervous jar to the spinal column, which has the effect, for the moment, of deadening sensibility (See Fig. 37). It creates a slight roaring in the ears, and the subject feels as if his senses were leaving him. It is at this moment that the professor calls out sharply and peremptorily, 'SLEEP! SLEEP QUICKLY! YOU ARE GOING FAST ASLEEP AT ONCE!' In very many cases this method is successful, and the subject's eyes roll back in his head, and he is forthwith in a condition of somnambulism."

Flower likewise gives another instantaneous method making use of this shock-fear technique; "Suddenly arrest the attention of the subject; startling him when he is looking for nothing of the kind. A silver pencil is as good an object as any other by which to induce this instantaneous hypnosis. The act is performed by suddenly thrusting before the subject's eyes some such bright object, and forcibly asserting that the subject cannot take his eyes from the object, and will be compelled to follow it wherever it is moved. Of course, if the subject had time to reason he would know that there was no power in a silver pencil which could attract him or draw him anywhere against his Will, but the operator gives him no time to reason, and immediately plies him with suggestions to the effect that he feels the pencil drawing him; that he cannot take his eyes off it; that he MUST follow it; and that it is useless for him to try to withstand its influence. It frequently happens that a glassy look will come over the eyes of the subject, and he moves forward in the direction in which the pencil is waved. As he moves, the operator lays his hands over his eyes, closes the lids, and says, 'You are wide awake, but you cannot open your eyes.' From this condition it is but a step toward the induction of somnambulism with all of its attendant phenomena."

Interesting and occasionally effective as these impulsive methods are, they cannot be overly recommended; not that they are especially injurious to the subject, but rather that they seem undemocratic, and tend to foster false impressions as to what Hypnotism really is. **Every Hypnotist should make it his rule to get the complete and willing consent of his subject to be hypnotized before ever attempting to induce the trance.** This is the American way of freedom of choice of action, and serves the purpose of helping to remove the superstitious fear which unfortunately hangs over even the word Hypnotism, itself, in the minds of some people.

Is it possible for a hypnotist to make a subject perform an immoral act?

On this question most modern authorities agree that a person's moral code under hypnosis remains largely unchanged. Remember, just because a person is hypnotized does not imply that he has become another individual in any sense whatsoever. What moral scruples the subject shows in his normal state of mind he will exhibit under hypnosis. Indeed, a hypnotized subject is often even more scrupulous than one awake, for the unconscious section of mind seems to have an innate sense of danger, and rallies quickly to the protection of the personality—either by deliberately awakening the subject from the trance, even in direct defiance of the commands of the operator, or by a deliberate refusal to perform the requested immoral suggestions.

Are women more easily hypnotized than men?

Not necessarily. The sexes are about equal in their all-over responsiveness to hypnosis. While the greater emotional intensity of women can frequently make them somewhat more susceptible to entering rapidly deep trance, unless they are motivated properly by the performer, this very emotional quality can produce a self-consciousness that is most resistant to earnest concentration on the performer's suggestions. Men, on the other hand, tend to accept the experience in a more matter-of-fact way, and more readily comply with directions.

SOME USEFUL SUGGESTIONS

Use Preliminary Experiments

In working with a group, before you try for any trance phenomena, always commence with some of the simple preliminary tests such as drawing the subject backward or forward, saying before you start that you are not going to hypnotize anyone now, but you simply wish to ascertain which of them are able to concentrate the most forcefully. Work with as many subjects as is possible in these first tests before trying to hypnotize. When all have tried who volunteer, pick out someone who seems the most susceptible, and subject him to the test of fastening the hands together. After you have successfully completed this test, you may perform others of this nature, and then proceed to induce the trance. But remember, do not try to put anyone to sleep until you have exhibited a number of minor tests, and dispelled completely the fear of Hypnotism.

Establish Confidence

Whenever possible, let a new subject see you hypnotize someone whom you have hypnotized previously before you try to influence him. This rapidly develops the potential subject's confidence in your ability to hypnotize, and shows him that there is nothing to fear in it.

Do Not Boast

Always approach your work in a modest, confident manner. To boast of your ability is to develop a challenging attitude in your subjects, and frequently invites failure to the successful culmination of your experiments.

Keep Your Promises

Never under any circumstances be so untrustworthy as to have your subjects do a single thing you have told them you would not do. Many subjects will request that, if they are hypnotized, you will not make them do such and such. When you give your promise to follow their wishes, always keep that trust.

Revolving the Head

The following process will sometimes hypnotize a person when other techniques fail. Place the fingers of your left hand on the back of the subject's head, pressing inward and upward at the base of the brain. Place the thumb of your right hand at the root of his nose and your fingers on his left temple. Now revolve his head very slowly in a small circle, as you present your "sleep formula."

Tapping on Top of the Head

Another effective technique for inducing sleep, is to gently tap on the top of the front part of the subject's head. Do this very lightly, but with a firm pressure, and at regular intervals like the ticking of a clock. Give suggestions of sleep during this tapping. If the subject becomes very sleepy, but does not quite lose consciousness, then let your fingers rest firmly on the top of his head, and tell him that soon he will be breathing very deeply, and will soon be snoring. Then commence yourself to breathe very deeply right beside his ear, and a little later let out a soft snore. The subject hearing this will frequently drop into a deep sleep at once.

Pressure Upon the Eyelids

When the eyes of the subject are closed, steady pressure applied at the corners of the eyes, near the root of the nose, will often assist in inducing sleep.

Suggestions Supplemented

When giving suggestions that the arms feel heavy, it is often well to press slightly down upon the arms, and when you tell your subject that everything is dark before him, put your hands over his eyes. Such devices to intensify the force of your suggestions are always valuable.

Combination of Methods

Hypnotism may be induced by suggestion, bright objects, or by passes. A combination of processes will usually hypnotize more persons than any single one device. After a person has once been hypnotized, suggestion is usually the only means that need be employed.

Increasing Susceptibility in the Trance

Before awakening your subject, give him the suggestion that the next time you attempt to hypnotize him that he will go immediately to sleep; that as he gazes into your eyes, sleep will come over him at once. Such post-hypnotic suggestions will greatly increase your ease in hypnotizing him at any later period.

Hypnotizing in Natural Sleep

Go very quickly to the sleeping person and speak to him in a very low whisper, saying, "Sleep, you are sound asleep. Do not be afraid, nothing will disturb you. You will not wake up, for you are going deeper and deeper down fast asleep. Sleep, sleepy, sleep." Repeat some such "sleep formula" several times. If you notice any signs of the person awakening, immediately desist; otherwise keep the suggestions up for three or four minutes; then put your hand on the subject's head and say to him, "You hear no sound except my voice, you are fast asleep." Now ask him some simple question, such as, "How do you feel?" or tell him that he smells a rose and ask if he smells its beautiful fragrance? Insist on a reply to your question until he answers it. When he does so without awakening, you may be assured that he is in the hypnotic state. You can now proceed to present whatever suggestions you desire. As you conclude, tell the subject to return to his normal, healthy sleep, and that he will not remember anything that has occurred. When he awakens the next morning, he will have no memory whatever of your suggestions.

Hypnotizing a Large Group at Once

Have your subjects sit in a semi-circle, stand out in front of them so they can all easily see you, and tell them to look directly at you. In the meantime, pass your eyes clear around the semi-circle, so that each person feels that you are looking directly at him. You can now proceed to work tests on the entire group exactly as you would with one subject. Having gained the attention of every person in the group, focus your gaze on no one person in particular, letting it rest about a foot above the head of your central subject, and give your suggestions very forcefully towards this focused space. Now tell them to put their hands together, to push on them tightly, and when you count "Three" they will be unable to pull them apart. Count, "One, two, three," and state emphatically, "Now you cannot take your hands apart. Try, try hard, but they will not come apart. All right now, when I snap my fingers they will instantly come apart." Snap your fingers and complete the test. If you wish to put them to sleep, stand out in front and tell them to close their eyes and to think of sleep, going sound asleep, and suggest, Close your eyes, tightly, think of sleep, your head feels heavy, you are going sound asleep, your limbs feel so heavy, so heavy they are pressing into the floor. You cannot move, you cannot feel anything. Your eyes are closed tightly, they will not open. You are sound asleep. You are fast, fast asleep, you hear nothing but the sound of my voice, and it is sending you down, down deeper and deeper to sleep. Proceed then as you think best, concluding the test by suggesting, "All right now, you have slept long enough. I will count slowly from one to five, and at the count of five you will all be awake, wide awake and feeling fine." Then count slowly from one to five. We will discuss in detail this subject of Group Hypnosis when we consider Stage Hypnotism.

Post-Hypnotic Suggestions

After you get your subject soundly to sleep, tell him very positively three times, that at some certain time he will do some particular thing. For example, suggest. "At one o'clock you will go down town and buy an ice cream cone and bring it back to me. You will not remember that I gave you this suggestion, but at one o'clock this very afternoon you will feel an over-whelming impulse, and you will go down town, buy an ice cream cone and bring it back to me." Be sure your suggestions are very positive and emphatic. After your suggestions are thus repeatedly given, awaken the subject, and, at the appointed time, he will do exactly as you instructed him; thinking that he is acting entirely of his own volition. Be very careful never to give the hypnotized subject post-hypnotic suggestions to carry out that are too difficult or dangerous for him to perform. You cannot be too careful of the character of the post-hypnotic suggestion that you give. The whole secret of this post-hypnotic influence consists in telling the subject, when he is in a deep hypnotic sleep, the thing you wish him to do when he awakens. Always repeat your suggestions several times so that they are strongly emphasized in his mind. If he should fail to carry out the suggestions, you may be sure that the failure is due to either lack of conviction in the way you presented your suggestions, or that the subject was not in a sufficient depth of trance for post-hypnotic effects.

Hypnotizing by Telephone

Use a subject whom you have previously hypnotized, and have him place the receiver to his ear. Have him seated so he can pass into the trance in comfort. Then suggest, "In half a minute you will be sound asleep. Already your head feels heavy. You are getting tired, so tired. Your eyelids are heavy, they are closing. You cannot stay awake, you are going sound asleep. Now you are sound asleep. Sleepy, sleep, sleep." By this time, the subject usually will be deeply sleeping. In this test, give your first suggestion very firmly and positively—"IN HALF A MINUTE YOU

WILL BE SOUND ASLEEP!"

Hypnotizing by Mail

Select a subject who is very responsive to your influence. Then write on a slip of paper in large letters, "In a few seconds after reading this you will be sound asleep. You can already feel yourself getting sleepy. You cannot stay awake. You are going fast to sleep. Go to sleep now." Then sign your name in big letters. When your subject opens and reads such a letter from you, he will drop into a deep trance. Needless to say, if when you previously hypnotized him you had given him a post-hypnotic suggestion to the effect that when he received such a hypnotic letter from you, that it would send him immediately down into the trance, it will increase the effectiveness of the test a hundredfold.

Transfer of Control

After you have hypnotized your subject, simply say to him positively, "You will now do whatever Mr. So and So tells you to do, and will obey every one of his suggestions just as you have mine." Have the third party then place his hand on the subject's forehead as you continue to suggest that the subject will now obey him.

Test of Sleep

Watch your subject closely. Usually when hypnosis comes there is a sort of drooping about the corners of the mouth. This is often coupled with a little intake gasp of breath, and the breathing becomes deep and regular as in sleep. Then gently lift up your subject's closed eyelid as you suggest that the action will send him down deeper and deeper into sleep. If he is deeply hypnotized, usually his eyeballs will be rolled upward under the upper lid. Incidentally, a relaxed mouth is a very good indication of a good hypnotic subject. Persons with tense lips should be avoided.

Taste and Sight

It is easier to deceive the sense of taste than it is the senses of sight and hearing. A suggestion that the subject experiences a bitter taste in his mouth is much more certain to work than one that he will see a beautiful mountain in front of him when he opens his eyes. This principle of progressively arranging the illusions from the simpler to the more complicated is important in developing a new subject.

Illusions Simpler to Produce than Hallucinations

It is easier to make a subject believe that one object is another object, than it is to make him believe that an object exists in empty space. For instance, you can make him see a blue carpet as a pond of water much more readily than you can an elephant in an empty room. Use this device of utilizing a stimulating object resembling the suggested illusion when first creating optical delusions.

Producing Anesthesia

If you prick your subject with a pin he will feel and react to it unless you suggest that a certain area of his skin is immune to all pain. Run your fingers over an area of his arm as you suggest, "All sensation is leaving your arm. It is numb and cold. You will feel nothing in it whatsoever." Then prick it with a sharp needle, and the puncture will be completely ignored if your subject is deeply hypnotized.

Producing Catalepsy

After you get the subject into a deep trance, have him stand up straight, and tell him that the muscles of his body are stiff and rigid, that they will not bend, no matter how much weight is placed on them. As you give these suggestions make passes over his body, pressing in here and there on the muscles of his arms. legs, and chest as though to tighten them, and say, "You are perfectly rigid." Then shout very loudly, "RIGID!" Your subject will become stiff like a pole and be utterly unable to bend in any direction. When you are ready to remove the cataleptic state, tell him to loosen his muscles, to relax himself, and when his muscles are again relaxed, awaken him gently from the trance.

Causing the Pulse to Beat Rapidly or Slowly

When your subject is in a deep hypnotic sleep, suggest to him that his pulse will begin to beat very, very rapidly when you reach the count of "Three." Then count, "One—Two—Three," and suggest, "Now your pulse is beginning to beat fast, faster, faster, faster, etc." Give the opposite suggestions to make it beat slowly. Do not under any circumstances give suggestion of this type to persons with heart ailments. Such subjects should be avoided in most hypnotic experiments.

Causing the Subject to Blush

Get him into a deep trance, and present the suggestions that he will blush, that his face will become red, etc. Then repeat some incident of embarrassment that will make him blush, and describe that the conditions around him are such as to make him blush. Such physiological experiments are very strong tests with which to convince a skeptical audience of the reality of your phenomena.

Keeping Other Persons from Influencing Your Subjects

If you do not wish anyone else to hypnotize your subject, simply put him into a deep sleep and tell him that he cannot be hypnotized by anyone but you, unless he say first the words, "ZAM, ZAM, ZAM" (or any word cue combination desired). This serves as a cue that the subject unconsciously waits for as the opening door to entering hypnosis. Never tell a subject just outright that he cannot be hypnotized again, as such might render him unsusceptible to all future experiments. If he thinks he is too susceptible, you might tell him that he cannot be hypnotized unless he, himself, expresses a wish to be.

Awakening with Upward Passes

Passes made in a downward direction are used to induce the trance, while passes made upward are used to remove it. Turn your palms upward, and starting about the subject's stomach move them upward past his face. Repeat these upward passes several times. Blowing gently on the closed eyelids is also useful in awakening the subject.

Awakening Difficult Subjects

Only rarely will you experience any difficulty in awakening the subject, but in such a case, say to him, "All right now, I want you to wake up. I know you are sleepy and tired, but you MUST wake up now. You have slept long enough. Tell you what I will do. I will count very slowly from one to ten, and when I reach the count of 'Ten' you wake up. Fair enough? Will you awaken at the count of ten?" If the subject does not answer, persevere until he does, and make him promise that he will wake up when you reach the count of "Ten." Then continue, "All right then, here goes. One, two, three, four, five, six, seven, eight, nine, ten." Just as you say "Ten" clap your hands loudly together (in the case of a subject of this type you need not worry about shocking his nervous system as he is the lethargic type, and you want lots of noise) and say, "WAKE UP! WAKE UP! ALL RIGHT, WIDE AWAKE NOW!" Keep striking your hands together, make upward passes, and give suggestions until the subject is fully awake. This process will awaken the most difficult subject.

Awakening a Subject Someone Else has Hypnotized

Occasionally, you may be called upon to dehypnotize a subject that some inexperienced operator has entranced. The method is to proceed to gain rapport with the subject by the process of hypnotizing him. Put your hand on his head and repeat "sleep formula" to him, then test him for response to your suggestions. After he has responded to a few tests, say very decidedly to him, "Now when I tell you to do anything you will do it at once." Then have him move around a bit to get active control of his mind. After this, apply the technique previously explained for awakening difficult subjects and he will awaken readily.

Awaken with Confidence

The only reason subjects are ever difficult to awaken is that they have lost confidence in the operator. A hypnotized person is often very sleepy, and to ask them to come immediately out of the trance sometimes seems just too much, and hence they make no attempt to obey you. But never for a moment lose confidence of your ability to awaken the subject. Remember, a hypnotized person is highly suggestible, and a betrayal of nervousness on your part over concern about awakening him is certain to be interpreted as a suggestion that it is difficult to awaken him. Simply be calm and collected, and keep in mind that a lack of confidence is as unfavorable to success in removing the trance as it is in producing it.

Practice! Practice! Practice!

You now have the material to make you an expert Hypnotist, but the skill with which you will apply that knowledge is entirely up to you. Hypnotism is exactly like Magic in that respect; a group of tricks do not make the Magician—it's how you interpret and present those tricks, that counts. So, practice diligently and develop your skill. Practice on single subjects. Practice on groups. Practice in private. Practice in public. Learn your hypnotic methods so thoroughly that they are second nature to you. Make your techniques as much a part of you as you have the card pass or some other favorite sleight, so that they occur almost automatically with complete smoothness and ease. Then, when you are so confident of your ability, step out, and you are ready for STAGE HYPNOTISM.

AN INTRODUCTION TO
STAGE HYPNOTISM

When you think about stepping out on a stage expecting to entertain a large audience for a period of from thirty minutes to a full hour, or possibly even longer, with nothing for support but a group of empty chairs, it is certainly an undertaking to make the stoutest showman pause and speculate. Indeed, it is the "worries" of such a presentation that has made stage demonstrations of Hypnotism the rare events they are. In fact, the qualifications for the successful stage Hypnotist rate among the top in the entertainment profession . . . for Stage Hypnotism can unquestionably be cited as one of the most difficult of all possible forms of entertainment to present, since the performer continually has to meet, deal with, and master the uncertainties of the **Human Equation.**

Unlike the Magician, who has his act entirely under the control of his own skill, the Hypnotist relies entirely upon the conduct of volunteers invited up from the audience itself. If the subjects respond, and he succeeds in producing hypnotic phenomena through them, fine—his show is a success. BUT, conversely, if his subjects do not respond—his show is a failure. And that is a big BUT!

Relying upon the responses of volunteers to put the show over is too great a risk to take, many performers will say. **But it can be done 100 per cent successfully,** and it is our purpose to show the necessary insights and techniques to make the stage presentation of hypnotism feasible and to reduce to its very minimum all possibilities of failure. For indeed, although in Hypnotism you must always deal with the unpredictableness of the human mind, the cards can be so "stacked" in your favor that the success of your show can be largely a certainty.

There are many advantages to the hypnotic act. The fact that it takes **skill** to present greatly raises its prestige and value. Then, too, it is spectacular and even production-size in scope. And yet, you need carry no props, or equipment—**the audience providing all of the material for your performance.** All the performer need bring with him is his knowledge, which, when artfully applied, can make towards the production of a show without parallel in audience favor. For Hypnotism has everything: comedy, mystery, drama; coupled with educational and thought provoking phenomena. So complete is the appeal of the hypnotic show that, properly handled, it is doubtful if any other entertainment is capable of creating more spontaneous interest and enthusiasm.

Are such goals worthy of cultivation by the Magician? If so, then practice and study well, for the presentation of Stage Hypnotism is a culmination of the skills of the lecturer, the psychologist, and the showman. Artfully blended they flow into the perfect hypnotic presentation that lifts STAGE HYPNOTISM from the novelty act class and places it among the Arts.

Now, the performance of Hypnotism upon the stage calls for, first, a thorough and basic knowledge of Hypnotism, and secondly an understanding of showmanship. **Remember, your job as a stage performer is primarily to entertain.** So while you naturally must be concerned with the induction of the hypnotic state, you must be even more concerned with the keeping, holding and building of the interest of your audience.

In view of the dual nature of the work, it obviously calls for a skilled craftsman, but to the man with the initiative to master the art, Stage Hypnotism indeed offers a most profitable field of entertainment.

Let us consider briefly, therefore, just what qualifications you will need to be a competent Stage Hypnotist. First, you must be thoroughly acquainted with your hypnotic technique, and have your knowledge ever ready for the skillful implanting of suggestions for the production of both waking tests and the deeper hypnotic phenomena.

Second, you must be a showman. By a showman is meant a qualified entertainer, and, as such have a good vocal delivery, poise, stage deportment, audience understanding, a sense of timing, dramatic ability; all are essentials that must form your background as a talented performer. **Remember, the ability to entertain is a skill that comes with practice, and the best teacher is experience.**

Third, you must have a routine. Nothing is so important to the Stage Hypnotist as to know **exactly** what he is going to do, what test follows next, and to proceed through the basic pattern of his show, from start to finish, with precision. The hypnotic show is very similar to the stage play; it has an opening, a body, a climax, and a conclusion. The exact drama of your particular show depends largely upon yourself, although as a hypnotic entertainment it is bound to flow along certain lines. **However, whatever your specific routine, it must be thoroughly learned and become second-nature to yourself.**

Lest it should seem that all of these "musts" for successful Stage Hypnotism loom somewhat over-whelming, let's pause a moment and consider a few of the factors that are working in your favor—factors that make the presentation of the hypnotic act not as difficult as it might at first appear.

In this regard, always realize that the stage presents a glamourized situation which automatically places you in a position of prestige. Your advance advertising, your introduction, the audience expectation to witness hypnotic miracles, your acceptance as a Hypnotist, the very fact that you are on the stage as the performer — you thus assuming the active role while the spectators have the passive or submissive are all factors very much in your favor right at the very start of the stage exhibition of Hypnotism. In other words, **prestige and expectation are working with you** —as a Hypnotist, you know what this means for the successful induction of hypnosis.

Now, just before we plunge directly into starting the hypnotic show, let's touch briefly upon a few underlying essentials of a good hypnotist, i.e., your appearance, your manner, your speech, and your delivery.

Remember, when you hypnotize you are in close contact with your subjects, so naturally your appearance is of the greatest importance and must stand-up under close scrutiny ... so have your clothes and toilet sparkling. **In other words, look attractive.**

Now as to your manner, you have to **sell** your suggestions so strongly that they will be unqualifiedly accepted in order to produce hypnosis, so, naturally, you cannot boast or challenge. Rather adopt the manner of the successful doctor. **Be quiet, reserved, dignified, direct, obviously completely confident in knowing your work, and always entirely the master of the situation.**

On your speech, **know your hypnotism so thoroughly and your routine so perfectly that every word flows out and carries instant conviction.**

As a stage hypnotist, you have a dual delivery to get over; one to the audience, and the other to your subjects. To the audience, your comments should be to the point, good natured (but never deliberately funny), and **presented much in the manner of an educated lecturer—not dry, but intelligent.** To your subjects, **your speech should be direct and positive.** There is a certain knack to the giving of suggestions that you, as a practicing hypnotist, undoubtedly have mastered. Generally speaking, your delivery is given in such a manner that, while it may often be very quiet in tone, it instantly carries conviction and demands acceptance.

Having so prepared yourself, and, armed with confidence in your ability to entertain and hypnotize— **assume the mental picture and knowledge that your subjects and your audience will react exactly as you plan they will. You are the leader and they must follow.** You are now ready to step forward to the front of the stage and further build-up your initial prestige with your **opening lecture.**

THE OPENING LECTURE

The **opening lecture** is vitally important to the success of the hypnotic show. It sells you, it sells your subject, it secures volunteers to hypnotize. Learn and deliver it well—**it has an important selling job to do.**

Since you are now at the point where you are studying Stage Hypnotism, let us assume that you have acquired the necessary background for the work, i.e., considerable practice with Hypnotism in private, are at home on the stage, know thoroughly what you are about and just what difficulties, hypnotically speaking, you have to contend with, and that you are prepared to meet and handle any situation that may arise. **In other words, that you are master of both your art and yourself.**

The average audience which the Hypnotist faces, is largely composed of three types of people: 1. **The skeptical unbeliever;** 2. **The curious, credulous witness** who believes in Hypnotism all the way from a mild acceptance to a superstitious awe; 3. **The casual observer** to whom your show is only a show that he hopes will prove amusing.

It is your job in your opening lecture, therefore, to even out these three types, and to set them all on a common ground by convincing the skeptic that you know your business and that there is really a great deal to the subject of hypnotism, by fascinating yet further the believers (for here, in this group, you can expect to find some of your best subject material), and by arousing the interest of the casual observer so that he will sit up with a, "Now I'm really going to see something" expression.

To meet these requirements your opening lecture must obviously be interesting, informative, and illustrative ... and do it all in a concise manner so that the audience has no chance to get bored while they await the actual experiments to commence. To this end, something like the following may fill the bill:

The curtain up, your stage set with its customary semi-circle of empty chairs, your introduction completed, you approach your audience with a confident, yet friendly, smile as you comment:

"Ladies and Gentlemen, with your kind attention I will present a number of scientific demonstrations in Hypnotism. Before I begin, a few explanatory remarks will not be out of place.

"Hypnotism is now in a stage of advancement and achievement. While in the past it was often greeted with skepticism, today, it is openly acclaimed, and is practiced by both medical doctors and university professors.

"As you are all undoubtedly aware, through the present popular articles on the subjects, Hypnotism is now thoroughly recognized as a science throughout the entire civilized world.

"Now, just what is Hypnotism? Hypnotism, according to the latest psychological findings, has been defined as an extension of concentration ... in other words, it is the rather remarkable power that ideas possess when they claim our complete attention. Such dominant ideas are called suggestive ideas.

"Here, let me give you an example of this power of suggestion, a very simple little experiment you can all easily try that nicely illustrates this force underlying Hypnotism.

"Everyone first sit back, relaxed in your chairs. That's it. Now place your feet flat on the floor, and let your hands rest comfortably in your lap. And now . . . direct your attention towards me and towards this yellow, juicy, bitter lemon. It's such a sour, bitter lemon. I take this knife and cut through its rind. Look at that juice, that sour, bitter juice dripping down to the floor. Now, I'm going to suck that sour, bitter lemon juice. (Suck it audibly). Say, **it is** bitter and tart. So sour! And as I suck it, notice how your mouths begin to fill with saliva—how they water!

"You're bound to feel it . . . and there, my friends, is an example of suggestion in a very simple form. How does it work? First, the lemon provides you with an idea—an idea of something sour. That idea becomes realized unconsciously in your mind, the salivary glands secrete, and your mouth fills with saliva . . . and there is the power of suggestion, the very force upon which Hypnotism is based.

"In a moment, I am now going to request a few volunteers to come up on the stage to occupy these chairs and to participate in some demonstrations in Hypnotism, I am sure you will find all of these experiments of great interest . . . and I assure you I shall treat everyone with the utmost courtesy and respect. I only request that those who come up on the stage be serious about experimenting with this wonderful state of mind, and that they be willing to concentrate intently upon the suggestions offered. With such co-operation, together we shall unquestionably secure some most remarkable phenomena.

"Without further ado now, I invite you my friends —yes, both ladies and gentlemen are welcome—to come forward and occupy these chairs upon the stage. Come on up, let us experiment with Hypnotism. Come up, come on up now. That's it, come on up."

So concludes your opening lecture as the volunteers commence treking up to the stage.

Let us pause, for a brief moment, before proceeding further, and see just where we stand now. First, your speech has acquainted your audience with you. It has further placed Hypnotism on its rightful pedestal as an accepted scientific fact. Secondly, you have given a logical explanation for the phenomena, and further presented an actual illustration of suggestion and shown how it works. The stunt with the lemon is bound to succeed, is very graphic and perfectly illustrates the power of suggestion.

Next, you have requested volunteers to come up on the stage to experiment with Hypnotism. Remember, you have not invited or challenged **any person** to come forward and be hypnotized by you—**your statements clearly request only those who are serious and who are willing and anxious to experiment with hypnotism to come forward.** Thus you have an "out" if later you have to send down any possible "wise guys" from the stage. You have called Hypnotism a state of advanced attention or concentration. Obviously, if persons will not co-operate and concentrate as you direct, no Hypnotism is to be expected . . . so you have perfectly safe-guarded yourself from the very start.

Statistics of hypnotic responsiveness show that one person out of five is a natural somnambulist—in other words, is a really good hypnotic subject. In situations of prestige, such as on the stage, you can very possibly increase that responsiveness . . . but there is another factor also very much in your favor. Somnambulists have a tendency to attend hypnotic programs, and your advance announcements of such seems to attract them like a light does moths. So you may be sure that your audience will be well stocked with its full share of such persons.

Now the trait of natural suggestibility is one of the chief characteristics of a good hypnotic subject— so suggestion goes to work immediately you ask for volunteers. First, there is a group of awaiting chairs with their implied suggestion that they must be filled. Then there are your suggestions to "Come up . . . come on up . . . come on up and volunteer." Over and over comes your request to come up and occupy those chairs; to come forward and experiment with Hypnotism. When it is practical, have a few persons "planted" in different parts of the hall, or theatre, to lead the way to the stage . . . these further amplify the suggestions **"to come on up."** It is a call that few natural somnambulists can resist. So up they come. **Thus, your committee will unquestionably contain a splendid representation of good subjects with which you can work.**

However, you protect yourself even further; as the volunteers come onto the stage, you greet each in turn with a shake of the hand and a square look in the eye. Right here you establish yourself as a warm human being. A human being who is to be respected, and whose instructions are to be followed.

Your committee now seated in a semi-circle facing you; what have you here? There is a group of persons entirely unknown to you. Again they are composed of three types of individuals: 1. **The natural somnambulists** (your really good subjects); 2. **The genuinely interested** (persons who will thoroughly co-operate with you and try their best to be hypnotized); 3. **The skeptics** (the "hypnotize me if you cans" and the "wise guys"). So far your approach has been to level out the

135

attitude of your audience, you must now further level out the attitude of this group upon the stage—and strive to get them all into a co-operative and working frame of mind. **So you comment, and lay the success of the whole performance deliberately in their laps:**

"The ability to be hypnotized is in reality a skill. And as a skill, it naturally requires some qualifications in order to be accomplished. Now, some persons seem innately to possess this amazing ability to enter hypnosis, while others have to develop it. It shall be my purpose this evening to help you pass into this remarkable state, or mood of mind, called Hypnotism."

What have you done? You've called the state of being hypnotized a skill—an accomplishment. To resist your influence is to admit they haven't "what it takes." Your skeptics are more or less on the spot . . . they had better follow along with you, or else, in the eyes of the entire audience, they admit their inadequacy. **That's the way to form the pattern of the successful stage hypnotic show.** It's never a challenge of your powers over the subjects . . . rather, you are the teacher—the teacher of a skill that those most qualified can achieve. **Remember, always make the entering of the hypnotic state seem an important thing**—an important achievement both in the eyes of your volunteer subjects and also in the eyes of the audience. **The entering of the hypnotic state must be "sold" as a worthy and a desired goal.** With your objective properly completed, your subjects should be in a frame of mind, that far from wishing to resist hypnotic influence has them actually anxious to see if they have the necessary skill to enter the state.

Several factors of the stage situation are working with you to help in fulfilling this objective. There is the audience which puts the subjects more or less in a keyed-up mood—in a sense they feel important, being on the stage as part of the show before all these spectators; while at the same time, they feel just a bit ill at ease and self-conscious. Then, there are the curtains, the lights, the music, **in fact, all the elements that go into the stage situation are working directly with you toward the placing of the volunteers in a mood receptive to suggestion and expectant of the approach of hypnosis.**

You will find that even when a volunteer comes up on the stage with a mind full of skepticism, it isn't so easy for him to continue to buck the tide of the stage situation, and that many will shortly slip into the path of the least resistance; **which path you are very carefully paving along directly into the desirability of entering the hypnotic state.**

There is definitely a pressure in the stage situation; you will feel it yourself. It is a sort of bond that unites the performer and the mass attention of the audience. You, as the performer, are in the situation as a leader, and as such it spurs you along. Your subjects, on the other hand, are in the situation in submissive roles, and every last one of them feels it, as it lulls them into a welcomed retreat to enter deep hypnosis— for that is what is expected of them and there they best fulfill the demands created in the immediate **stage situation.**

See how it is? Although the presentation of Hypnotism on the stage may at first seem a task almost too risky to attempt with any promise of success, handled with intelligence it soon shapes itself up into a situation that you, as a Hypnotist, will recognize as most desirable for the induction of hypnotic phenomena. At the same time, you will greatly appreciate the need for a thorough mastery of your subject and the careful routining of your demonstrations.

Before we proceed to the conducting of actual hypnotic tests upon the stage, let us consider a couple of alternative opening approaches to your hypnotic act.

The Opening Lecture combined with the "Itching Sensation Test" earlier described in this book forms another excellent introduction to your show. Study it well.

Yet another technique, that has been used with splendid success by some operators, utilizes a **suggestive test on the whole audience**, and then incorporates a culmination of the test that requires the subjects to come forward to the stage—thus illustrating the power of suggestion and at the same time securing your committee of volunteer subjects.

In the performing of this exciting experiment when you reach the point in your lecture for a demonstration, you tie it in as follows:

"Here, let me give you all an example of this power of suggestion. Every one relax back in your seat, place your feet flat on the floor and rest your hands in your laps. Now, close your eyes. Close them together tightly. Very tight, tight. Now, with your eyes closed, roll your eyes up, up under your closed eyelids, and look backwards, back into your very brain. Squeeze your eyes together tighter . . . now they are becoming stuck. The lids are becoming stuck together Stuck so tight. So tight! Soon it will be impossible to open them. They are stuck together so tightly—they just won't open. They're stuck tight together. That's it, keep looking back into your very brain. Your eye lids are stuck tightly together. They simply won't open, no matter how you try. Try hard! Hard! See they won't open!"

Watch your audience at this point. Many will struggle to open their eyes, but in vain. Their eyes are stuck tight shut. After a moment of fruitless attempts to open their eyes, suddenly clap your hands loudly and say,

"All right, all right, it's all gone. Look at me. You can now open your eyes. Open your eyes!"

This test is a safe one to work as an opening experiment since the small muscles about the eyes are very susceptible to suggestive influence. This coupled with the physiological fact that when the eyeballs are turned upwards under the closed lids—**as long as the eyes so remain looking upward it is physically** impossible to open the lids anyway (See Fig. 38).

FIG. 38

Having completed the "Eye Sticking Test," follow right along to a second experiment in suggestion with,

"Such is the power of suggestion. You see, the greater your ability to concentrate, the more powerful are the effects produced by your mind."

There is psychology in the above lines, viz, **response to your suggestions proves an indication of the audience's ability to concentrate**. You continue:

"Let us all now try another simple test. This time

the fastening of the hands together. Everyone raise your arms above your head. That's it. Now turn your palms so they face each other and spread your fingers wide apart. Now, place your hands together and interlock your fingers. Interlock your hands tightly together. Squeeze tightly. Tight!"

As you comment, illustrate the procedure by raising your own hands above your head, and interlocking your fingers tightly (See Fig. 39), say:

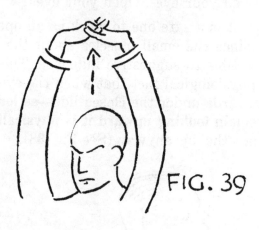

FIG. 39

"Now, turn your hands outward and upward. That's it, turn your palms upward and stretch out your arms straight above your head. Squeeze your fingers together tightly . . . very tightly. So tight. Keep your attention firmly concentrated on me. Those arms are becoming stiff. Push them up stiff . . . stiff! Your arms are becoming stiff and tense, and your hands are becoming tightly locked together. Stuck tight together. Stuck so tightly they simply will not come apart no matter how hard you try. They are stuck tight! Keep pushing your arms up stiff, so very stiff. Your fingers are stuck together, your hands are glued together. So tight. See you cannot pull them apart. Try and pull them apart. You cannot! They simply will not come! They are stuck!"

Again watch your audience carefully, and observe their reactions. Some will take their hands apart when you say, "Try and pull them apart." Others will find their hands stuck firmly, so firmly that they only come apart after considerable effort. **While still others will have their hands stuck together so tightly that all of their efforts fail to separate them.** These latter you address,

"Please step forward to me here at the foot of the stage, and I will release your hands for you."

Down the aisles they come, hands locked over their heads. Each in turn you gaze in the eyes, and with a firm command state, "It is all gone now. Unlock your hands. You can now. Relax your arms. Your hands are free!"

One by one their stuck hands will come free, but you do not let them go back to their seats, rather with a gesture you request them to go up on the stage and occupy the chairs.

Just released from the suggestive influence of the "Hand Locking Test," and now up front before the audience, the subjects have little alternative other than to comply . . . **so you shortly have your chairs filled, and, what is most important, filled with all good subjects.**

This test, as just described, works splendidly incorporating as it does both the suggestive factor as well as the physical one that when the fingers are so interlocked with the palms turned upward above the head, **so long as the arms are held stiff and straight up, as you instruct, it becomes almost a physical impossibility to release the hands anyway.**

Of course, it depends largely upon your style of working, but in the majority of cases thus conducting tests on the entire audience is to be avoided; since they cannot possibly be 100 per cent universally effective, the spectators upon which they did not work are bound to be somewhat questioning as to why they were not influenced while others were. Naturally, you can explain it logically on the basis of stronger concentration on the part of some, but it's an emotional questioning, all of which tends to put your subjects in a class apart from the rest of the audience which is one of the very effects you most wish to avoid. The impression you are striving to create being that hypnotic responsiveness is a universal phenomenon common to all . . . the audience being led to identify themselves with the subjects on the stage with the feeling that if they were up there, that they, too, would be reacting similiarly.

Obviously, therefore, if a test is performed on the entire audience, those persons on which it falls tend automatically to drop out of rapport with the subjects on the stage. But such may well be counterbalanced by the opportunity such group tests afford to secure rapidly the very best hypnotic subjects from amongst those in the audience. It's an arbitrary question, so use your own judgment.

You now have ample material with which to form an extremely effective and adequate Opening Lecture. So prepared, you are ready to tackle the main body of the hypnotic show.

THE HYPNOTIC SHOW

Your subjects seated in a semi-circle before you, first address them as follows:

"On behalf of the entire audience, I wish to thank you ladies and gentlemen for so kindly volunteering. I shall do my very best to make your stay here on the stage more interesting."

Turn then and address the audience, "And friends in the audience, kindly pardon my back as I must turn from time to time to address the committee during the hypnotic experiments. And please, at the beginning of these experiments, please refrain from laughing as this disturbs the subjects here on the stage in their efforts to properly concentrate. After we have proceeded for a space, you may laugh as freely as you wish, but at first, please remain quiet, and witness the demonstrations as quiet observers . . . thus you will be extending to these friends upon the stage the same courtesy that you, yourself, would desire were you up here in their places."

First Group Experiment — "Hypnotic Mood Test"

Turn half way about and address the committee, "In our first experiment now, we shall produce what is called the hypnotic mood. It is a mood of rest, of calm, of relaxation. First, everyone sit back comfortably in your chairs, place your feet flat on the floor, and rest your hands in your lap, each hand resting separately on each knee (See Fig 40). That's fine. Just adjust yourselves in your chairs so that you will be perfectly comfortable.

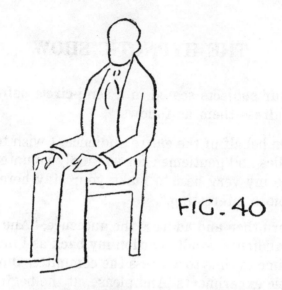

FIG. 40

"Now, everyone direct your complete and undivided attention towards me, and pay close attention to every suggestion and idea I give you. Now, the ability to be hypnotized is a skill that you can develop with practice, and it is our purpose here on this stage to practice together the development of this skill."

Watch your subjects carefully, and make everyone give you his undivided attention. This is most important; **be sure you have complete attention, exactly as you desire it, before you proceed any further.** Then continue.

"Now, to be hypnotized you must be able to relax while at the same time you are concentrating intently, so we shall relax progressively, step by step . . . and as I give you these thoughts to think about, concentrate like this: For example, if I should say that your arms are becoming heavy and that your hands are pressing down into your lap, think to yourself that your arms **are** getting heavy and that your hands are pressing down into your lap . . . and, as you do so, you will actually find that your arms and hands do feel heavier just as is being suggested.

"All right then, everyone think first of relaxing the muscles of the top of the head—the scalp." Place your hands on top of your scalp to emphasize the suggestion. "And as you concentrate on relaxing these muscles, you will begin to feel a tingling sensation coming into them; a gentle tingling sensation coming over your scalp. Now let your thought wander down over your face and relax those muscles. Relax the muscles about your mouth—relax completely. Now relax the muscles of your neck and shoulders, down through your chest. Relax every muscle of your body, right down through your thighs, your legs, down to your very feet. It feels so good to thus relax your body. And as you relax your body, your mind, too, begins to get relaxed and calm, and your eyes feel heavy. Those eyelids are so tired and heavy. They want to close. I will count now from one to three, and at the count of 'Three' everyone close your eyes, and relax completely. All ready! One—two—three. Close your eyes. That's it, everyone close their eyes down tight."

Watch the subjects closely, and if anyone does not close their eyes point directly at them, and say, "Close your eyes. Close them right down tight." **Make sure all eyes are closed before you continue,** "Now with your eyelids closed tight, roll your eyes back upward under the closed lids. Look back upwards toward the very center of your head. Roll your eyes back, and keep staring into your very brain. Your eyes are getting stuck together, stuck so tightly together that they simply will not open. Squeeze your eyes tighter together. They are stuck so tightly together they simply will not open try as hard as you will. Keep looking back into your brains, and try and open your eyes. You cannot. Those eyelids are stuck, they will not open try as hard as you will."

Here you are applying the "Eye Fastening Method" as described in the Opening Lecture chapter. Your subjects will strain in vain to open their closed lids, which is very important as it convinces them that actually some subtle influence is working over them; follow immediately on.

"Forget about your eyes now, just rest quietly in blackness, and let that relaxation seep through every fibre of your being. It feels so good, so calm, so restful. And now you are beginning to get drowsy. Let yourself just drift; becoming drowsy and sleepy. I will count slowly from one to ten. With every count you will become drowsier and drowsier, and sleepier and sleepier. Let yourself just drift, drifting down to pleasant rest. One-two—you are getting so sleepy and drowsy. Three—getting so relaxed. Let your head fall forward if you wish. Let every muscle relax completely. Four-five-six. Getting so calm and relaxed. So drowsy and sleepy. Let yourself just drift, down to sleep, pleasant rest. Seven-eight-nine. Let yourself just drift down towards sleep and rest. Every muscle so relaxed. Ten! Now pay close attention to every suggestion that I give you. As you rest there all calm and quiet, your mental processes are becoming intensified, becoming keyed up, so that you will find you can concentrate easily and powerfully upon every suggestion that I give you. You will find that you can easily accomplish every demonstration you try, and follow perfectly every suggestion that I give you. You are resting calmly and quietly. Nothing will disturb you, and you will find that you can concentrate intently upon every suggestion that I give you, and easily follow every one."

Throughout all of your demonstrations on the stage, make generous use of your hands as you talk, performing graceful, rhythmic passes out from the sides of your head in gentle sweeps towards your committee (See Fig. 41). These tend to hold the interest of both the subjects and the audience on you.

FIG. 41

"All right now, I shall count slowly from one to five. With every count you will begin to arouse yourself, and by the time I reach five you will all be active and alert. Ready, one-two-three—that's it, open your eyes now—four—all active and alert and ready to proceed to more advanced experiments. Five! Open your eyes everyone."

This first experiment is most vital to the success of your entire program. To the audience, it appears merely as an interesting beginning experiment. The eyes sticking, the subjects slumping down in their chairs and nodding about all tends to make them think that you are starting your program right off with a demonstration in group hypnotism. But actually you are accomplishing far more than this.

Notice in presenting the test you do not mention that you intend to hypnotize, but rather that you will show the committee how to enter the hypnotic mood of relaxing while concentrating. Thus you avoid any possible challenge from any of the subjects resisting, and if some one or two do not respond it makes little difference. But even though you are not deliberately hypnotizing, still your every suggestion is designed to lead your subjects progressively into a mild hypnotic state, first through relaxing, then the eye sticking, and lastly through suggestions of drowsiness, rest and sleep. During this process you accomplish several things: You can see which of your subjects are the most responsive. You can see which of them are the most resistive, and knowing the routine you intend to present, with a practiced eye, you can almost tell right at this point which subjects would be best to use in the various tests you plan to use. You have relaxed and calmed the group down from any tendencies of becoming boistrous, and **you have set in their minds suggestions leading to their ready acceptance and following of your every experiment.**

You can see how very important this first experiment is, so take your time with it, and get the group relaxed and very drowsy. Although many in your audience will think that you have hypnotized the entire committee, very few will actually have gone to sleep, but this is unimportant. **Your program is but beginning, yet through this very first step you have very well stacked the cards in your favor for the total success of your entire show.**

Now address your audience, "We are now ready for some actual experiments illustrating the power of suggestion . . . first, affecting the sense of balance. Who would like to be the first subject for this experiment?"

Falling Backward Test

Turn and look over the committee, select a subject that followed your instructions well in the previous experiment so that you can feel certain that he will respond equally positively to this test. **This is your first individual experiment and it is important that it succeeds** . . . but by now you know pretty well which persons among the group are most susceptible, so you are safe in your selection.

Always use a young man in this experiment, have him step forward, and ask him in a friendly fashion if he is perfectly willing to try the test. When he agrees, instruct him.

"All right then. Stand facing me with your feet side by side together. That is fine. Now in this experiment we are going to demonstrate how thoughts can actually influence the sense of balance as you concentrate. In a moment, I will stand behind you, and you will feel an impulse to fall right over backward. Now, have no fear of falling, as I will be right behind you and will catch you. All ready?"

As you give these directions, look him steadily in the eye, and in a soft, confidential manner request him to keep his mind intent on the ideas you will give him and to concentrate intently. When his eyes become fixed and steady on yours, compliment him by saying, "Fine, you concentrate splendidly." Now tell him to close his eyes, and to relax his body. Place your hand on his shoulder moving him a bit backward and forward to make certain that he is properly relaxed; tell him to imagine himself as a plank of wood hinged to the floor, and that he can sway easily in either direction, backward or forward, then say,

"All ready now, I will step behind you, and you will feel an impulse pulling you right over backward toward me. Have no fear of falling; I will catch you. All ready now, close your eyes and shut out the light."

Then softly to the subject confidentially say, "Let yourself go and don't resist. Let yourself come right back towards me as you concentrate on the influence pulling." **These little intimate asides to the subject are most important.** The audience only hears the major portions of your comments that describe and explain the experiment, but the subject receives full benefit of your confidence that tend to make him feel very much obligated to properly perform his portion of the experiment.

Now step behind your subject, touch lightly the back of his head so he will know that you are behind him, and start suggesting,

"You begin to feel an impulse pulling you right over backward. Concentrate your thoughts on falling over backward. Falling backward. You are falling back, back, right over backward. Have no fear of falling, I will catch you."

As you give these suggestions, draw your hands back from his body (See Fig. 42). To the audience it looks exactly as if some strange "force" from your hands were pulling him right over backward. And soon he falls directly over into your arms. You catch him, and at once assist him to regain his feet.

FIG. 42

**Here is a very important piece of business in han-
dling this test.** If you were to stand behind your subject and commence at once your drawing passes, **and
he did not fall over,** then you are "on the spot" as having failed in your very first individual test. **And a failure at this point in your show is very bad indeed.** So, as
you first give your suggestions of falling over backward, after you touch the back of his head, do not
stay behind the subject, rather step to his side, then
either cross your arms unconcernedly or let them rest
quietly at your sides, and commence your suggestions
of falling back, back, backward very quietly. **Then, as
he starts to fall, and then only, step behind him and
commence your mysterious pulling passes,** catching
him as he falls. You see by using this subtlety, from
the audience's point-of-view you have not even yet
started your experiment until you step behind the subject and commence the passes to draw him over backward. Thus, if it appears that he is not relaxed suffi-

ciently, or is deliberately resisting your suggestions, you can stop the proceedings before going any further and explain to him the all importance of his concentrating, not resisting, and letting himself respond freely. Or if he should prove entirely too unco-operative (which is very rarely the case since you have had such a good opportunity to select a suitable subject) you can even send him back to his seat, and select another subject for the experiment. **This principle of basically conducting two shows at the same time—one for the spectators and the other for the subject or subjects is an important factor to consider in the staging of the hypnotic show.**

Your subject having fallen backward, and again returned to his seat, you can say to him, "It felt just like a force of some kind pulling you right over backward, didn't it?" The subject confirms. Here you further establish the audience's impression that you actually drew the subject over through the application of some "force," and have also prepared the other subjects, on the stage, to further respond.

Now select another male subject and repeat the test. Next perform it with a girl. If possible select a girl who is not wearing high heels as these tend to shift her balance forward and make it very difficult for her to fall over backward. The use of a girl adds a little variety to the repeated tests, and gives the boys down front something to whistle over. By and large, however, conduct your individual tests on male subjects, using the girls only in group experiments, or tests where several subjects are involved at the same time.

Next take another male subject and draw him over backward. If he responds well; making it seem as though it were an afterthought, hold on to him, and keep him beside you as you explain to the audience.

"Now, many people seem to feel in witnessing these experiments that a person just tends naturally to fall over backward. Such is not true, and to prove it is not, let us reverse the experiment and try it, this time falling towards the front. You see, the influence works in any direction, backward, forward, or to the sides.

Falling Forward Test

You then stand your subject, with his feet together up before you, ask him to keep his eyes open this time and stare directly into your right eye; while you in turn gaze into his. Then raise your hands up in position opposite the sides of his head, and suggest, "You will begin to feel an impulse to fall forward . . . swaying forward right over towards me. Let yourself come, I will catch you. Falling forward. Forward. Right over forward."

As you give these suggestions, draw your hands in passes away from him, and slowly draw your body backward and downward (See Fig. 43). He will follow your eyes, and as you draw back will sway forward, and topple right over into your arms. Catch him, and immediately help him to his feet.

The Sitting Test

Since this subject has previously responded to the "Falling Backward Experiment," you are safe in assuming that he will respond to this related test of "Falling Forward," and, before he can return to his seat, you immediately follow through with yet another experiment. Have a chair brought center stage, and ask him to be seated. Then you address both the subject and the entire committee.

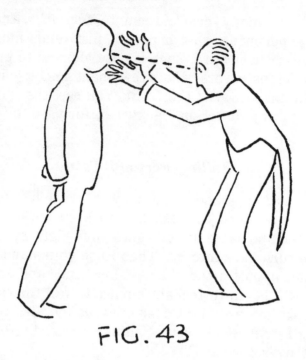

FIG. 43

"To save time in working this test upon each of you individually, we will all try an experiment together. So watch this next test very carefully; then, in just a moment, we will all perform it together." Then ask your subject to stand up directly in front of his chair with his feet together, and explain,

"In this test you will feel an impulse not only pulling you over backward, but your knees will come forward, and you will sit right back down in that chair." Then ask the subject to close his eyes, and commence making passes, pushing out from the sides of your face in toward him, as you suggest.

"All ready you begin to feel an impulse pulling you over backward. You are going to fall right back your knees are bending forward, and you are going to sit right back down in that chair. Sit down in the chair. Sit down. You are swaying backward, sitting down. Sit down. Sit down. Sit down!" Bend in closer and closer to your subject as you give these suggest tions (See Fig. 44). and he will shortly sway and suddenly sit down in the chair with a thump! Thank hir for his help, and let him return to his chair in the group.

FIG. 44

Second Group Experiment — The Sitting Test

Now address the committee, "All right now, let you all try that experiment. Everyone stand up right in front of their chair. That's fine. Place your feet together, and let your hands relax down at your sides. Now, one thing is very important, be sure your chair is right behind you. All right everyone, stand relaxed. now, directly in front of your chair. Now there is a large group here on the stage, so obviously I cannot work individually with each of you, but you can work individually with me. So forget all about the others near you. Forget all about the audience. Consider this an experiment just between you and me. All right, now close your eyes."

Your back is towards the audience, you are facing the committee, commence making passes out from the sides of your head in sweeps pushing toward the group as you did in the previous group experiment (See Fig. 41), and suggest, "In a moment, you will begin to feel that swaying impulse to fall right over backward, and sit right down in your chairs. All ready you begin to feel that swaying. Going over backward. Losing your balance and falling back, back, backward. Let yourselves go right along with it. Swaying back, back. backward. Your knees are coming forward, you are falling backward, and sitting right down in your chairs. Sit down. Sit down in your chair. Sit down!"

By this time many will have started to sway, and as you continue your suggestions some one or two persons will suddenly fall back in their seat with a thump. And this "thump" of the first subject falling will start others . . . and down they go, falling back with thuds into their seats, until almost everyone in the group finds himself unceremoniously seated. Some few of the subjects may possibly still be left standing, and, if so, merely request them to open their eyes and have a seat as you graciously gesture. This they do, feeling a little foolish at finding themselves the only ones standing while all the rest are seated. You immediately turn to the audience and comment,

"You see here an interesting example of the variability in response to suggestion. Some of the subjects felt the effects almost immediately, others not quite so rapidly, and some few not at all. Now why? Well, the reason lies entirely in the degree of the concentration on the suggestions given that each subject manifests." Turn so you are facing half way towards your subjects so that they too, can get the full benefit of your next words, "You see, you must concentrate to your very utmost if you are to acquire this skill of mastering your body with your minds." Here you again hammer home the necessity of full attention and concentration, and motivate the subjects yet further to try even harder in the experiments yet to follow.

This group sitting test is very important for it gives you a chance to again size up your subject's responses. **Note in what order they fall back in their chairs.** The ones that respond the best are the subjects you are going to especially select for the next group of tests.

Hand Fastening Test

You come now to the test of "Fastening The Hands Together," and it is here used as an transition experiment to more advanced demonstrations.

Address the audience, "We will now try some more difficult experiment in the power of suggestion; this time upon the muscles themselves."

Turn to your committee, point to the subject who fell down in his chair the most rapidly in the preceding tests, and ask, "Will you help me, please?"

The subject comes forward and takes a position

near the front of the stage with his left side towards the audience, facing you, and you explain, "We are now going to lock the hands together so firmly that they will not come apart no matter how hard you try to pull them apart."

Then say to the committee, "Everyone of you please watch this experiment very closely, because in just a moment we will try this test with you all together."

You will notice how the routining of these tests is psychologically handled, so that one demonstration **sells the one next to follow.** Your subject here now feels that he is setting an object lesson for the group, and hence feels responsible that he must do a good job. The group, on the other hand, become expectant of shortly trying the test themselves, and when they see it work on the subject, they are rendered all the more expectant of it working on them likewise.

Tell your subject now to look directly into your right eye, as you gaze back into his. Watch his eyes closely, if they wander in the least, command him to keep them firmly fixed on yours, and when they become set, compliment him softly with, "Splendid, you concentrate wonderfully."

Now suggest loudly, "All right, raise up your hands and interlock the fingers thus." Illustrate the procedure by interlocking your own, and holding your hands outstretched in front of you, continue, "That's it. Now press your hands tightly together. Squeeze them together with all of your might. Squeeze them tight, tighter, tighter! Those hands are getting stuck tightly together now." Continue illustrating the procedure by pressing your own hands tightly together (See Fig. 45). Then as you proceed, separate your hands and make gentle passes down his arms from the elbows to the hands. Squeeze his arm muscles here and there as you suggest,

FIG. 45

"Your hands are tense and tight. All of your muscles are tense and tight." Take his hands in yours, and press them tighter and tighter together as you say, "Those hands are getting locked tighter and tighter together, so tight they simply won't come apart, no matter how hard you try. I will count from one to three, and at the count of three, you will find you cannot pull your hands apart no matter how hard you try. Your hands are locked tight, tight together." Keep your eyes firmly fixed on his and slowly back away about six feet from him as you count, "One—two—three." Then increase the force and tempo of your suggestions saying very positively, "Those hands are locked fast together! They won't come apart! See how they stick! Pull on them! Pull on them with all of your might, but they won't come apart! They are stuck. They won't pull apart no matter how hard you try. Pull! Pull! Pull with all of your might!"

The subject will pull and struggle, but his hands will resist all of his efforts. Some subjects will try to separate their hands so violently that they actually become red in the face. Keep your eyes intently on the subject as he starts to pull on his hands, but after you see that they are powerfully stuck, you can deliberately turn your gaze away, and leave him entirely on his own.

After he has struggled for a time, approach him and say, "All right now. When I snap my fingers beside your ear your hands will instantly come right apart. All ready now." Snap your fingers, and his hands immediately separate. Thank the subject, and have him return to his seat as you address the group.

Third Group Experiment — Hand Locking

"All right now, let's all try the experiment together. Now remember this test is a definite challenge to your powers of concentration; the more powerfully you can concentrate, the better it will succeed. So let's all try hard for one hundred per cent results.

"Everyone ready? That's it, sit back in your chairs, place your hands in your lap, and look directly at me. Now everyone raise up your hands and interlock the fingers together thus." Again illustrate by doing it yourself. "Push your arms right out straight in front of you, and squeeze your hands tightly together. Keep your eyes firmly fixed on mine, and concentrate with all of your might."

Run your eyes rapidly from one end of the semicircle to the other, then as you start your actual suggestions focus your gaze at a point, about a foot above the head of the center subject, on the back curtain, and direct your suggestions forcefully towards that spot. This seems to produce an effect of abstraction that holds the attention of the entire group on yourself much better than were you to shift your gaze constantly about from one person to another, or if you were to select some especial subject for your focus of attention. Having the attention of all on you, commence your "Hand Locking" suggestions, getting more and more forceful as you proceed, climaxing your suggestions with, "I will now count from one to three, and at the count of three those hands won't come apart no matter how hard you pull! One—two—three! Your hands are locked tight! They won't come apart! Pull on them! They won't come apart! They are locked tight! Pull on them! PULL! PULL! PULL!" Use the familiar sweeping passes, out from the sides of your head, in towards the committee as you have in all of your group tests; these passes greatly assist in holding the attention of everyone riveted towards you.

The subjects in the group struggling to release their hands, you rapidly go to the right end of the semi-circle, and, one by one, release their hands with a rapid clap of your hands, and the suggestion, "All right, all right. It's all gone now. Relax and take your hands apart."

In place of the method of Hand Fastening just described, you can substitute the method given in the Opening Lecture chapter of turning the interlocked hands palms upward and raising the hands straight up above the head. This method is more certain of positive results as a test unto itself, but since you wish to avail yourself of this experiment as a further means of locating which of your subjects are responding best, so you can properly select your best material for subsequent tests, it is often wise to make use of the direct suggestive technique without any help from physiological principles.

The Open Mouth Test

As you are thus releasing the hands, when you come to an unusually good subject who is tugging extremely violently, first release his hands, and then quickly say to him, "Open your mouth, open it wide. Wide! Wider! Your jaw is getting stuck! Your mouth muscles are all getting tight and tense!" As you give these suggestions, make stroking passes from his cheekbones down under the chin, and press in on the jaw. Make your suggestions very rapidly, staccato, and forceful, as you say, "Your jaw is set. Your mouth is stuck open. You cannot close your mouth. Try to close it. You cannot close it."

Since you are standing right in front of the subject, no one but yourself can see what is going on, so if he should happen to resist the suggestion and close his mouth no harm is done, but if his mouth sets firmly open, back instantly away about ten feet as you point your outstretched finger at him. This is a "howler" for the audience. From right where you are standing, snap your fingers and say, "All right now, you can close your mouth," and it will close suddenly with a snap. Go immediately back to your process of releasing the hands of your group. When you come to another good subject, repeat the test of sticking his mouth open, and then finish releasing the hands.

The effect of this experiment must appear as though you suddenly had an inspiration to perform it, and work it very rapidly right in the midst of the process of releasing your subjects' hands. It is sensational!

Fourth Group Experiment — Fingertip Sticking

Your performance is now beginning to take on tempo and speed, **so keep that pace going.** Ask the whole group next to raise up their hands in front of them and place the tips of their forefingers together (See Fig. 46). Tell them to center their eyes on their fingertips, and to press them tighter and tighter together, then suggest,

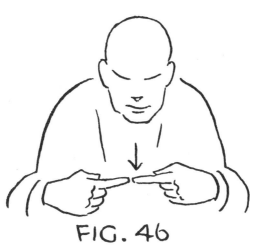

FIG. 46

"Now your fingertips are getting stuck tighter and tighter together. They are glued to one another. You cannot pull them apart no matter how hard you try. They are stuck, glued tight. Try hard to pull them apart, but they will not separate!" Give your suggestions for this test in a rapid, forceful manner. After the members of the committee have struggled to separate their fingers for a few moments, say, "All right, everyone look at me. Forget about your fingers. They will **come** apart now." Clap your hands, and apart they come.

You will find, as you get your performance rolling and your subjects under control, that you can increase the speed of performing each test. Less and less actual suggestive formulas need be employed, and you can become more and more commanding in the giving of your suggestions.

Fifth Group Experiment — Fingertip Missing Test

"Now, everyone hold your fingers about six inches apart. Those fingers are getting so nervous that you simply cannot make them meet no matter how hard you try. Those fingers simply will not meet. See how they miss, how nervous they are. They simply will not meet. Try and bring the tips together. See how they miss. Try hard, but they always miss. Try hard!" (See Fig. 47). As you give these suggestions, emphasize them by holding your own fingers apart and making them miss as you try to bring the tips together. When the whole committee is excitedly striving to make their fingertips touch, suddenly clap your hands, and say, "All right. All right. It's all gone. Your fingers will meet now."

FIG. 47

Always use this experiment as a follow up to the

"Fingertip Sticking Test." Having just experienced a previous phenomenon on their fingertips, the subjects are in the proper mood for it. The two tests dovetail together perfectly.

Sixth Group Experiment — Hand Shaking Test

Now turn to your audience and say, "Let us next try for a demonstration in automatic movements." Then again face your committee, and ask them to hold up their hands, let them dangle from the wrists, and shake them rapidly (See Fig. 48). Demonstrate this violent shaking and flopping about of the hands yourself, as you suggest, "That's it, shake your hands. Shake them faster and faster. Let them shake and flop free on your wrists. Shake them faster and faster. Now forget all about your hands. The movement is becoming automatic. You cannot stop it! Those hands are shaking all by themselves! You cannot stop shaking! Those hands will not stop shaking!"

FIG. 48

The Leg Shaking Test

Go up directly to one of the subjects who is shaking his arms very violently, grasp his leg at the knee, and bounce it up and down a few times as you suggest rapidly, "Your leg too is shaking. Shaking! Shaking! You cannot stop that shaking." Perform this test with a few other subjects.

The pace of your show is so rapid by now, that many of your subjects will be nearly exhausted from shaking, and your audience nearly collapsed from laughter. Rapidly dash down the semi-circle, from one shaking subject to another, releasing each with a clap of the hand and the suggestion, "All right now, it's all gone. It's all gone!"

You are now ready to change the tempo of your show back to a more moderate pace, as you address the audience, "You see these experiments upon the stage, and unquestionably they are unusual, but perhaps you wonder just what actual value they do have. This power of suggestion has been used for the correcting of many forms of neurotic difficulties and bad habits, such as stuttering for example. Let me show you through an actual experiment how quickly it can induce the condition of stuttering, and then as rapidly remove it."

Stuttering Test — Mouth-Locking Test — Name Amnesia

Select some subject who has been responding well to all of your tests, yet one whom you have not previously used. Whenever it is possible, it is aways best to use a different subject for each individual experiment, otherwise the audience may begin to feel that certain subjects are working in collaboration with you if you pick them from out of the group too frequently.

Have your subject seated in a chair as you lean over him, standing in close to his left side (See Fig. 49). Ask him to look up into your eyes, and suggest that his gaze is becoming fixed to yours. Watch his eyes, and when that fixed expression of fascination begins to creep into them, ask him to repeat the word, "MISSISSIPPI." This he does, and you say, "Now you will find that you cannot again utter that word without stuttering over it, no matter how hard you try. You cannot say Mississippi without stuttering. You cannot say it without stuttering. You will stutter. Misssssissssipppi. You cannot say Misss—issippi without stuttering. Try and say it."

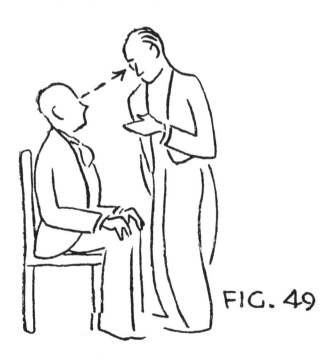

FIG. 49

Once you have your subject started, he will stutter all over the place on the word. Then softly say, "All right, you can pronounce the word clearly now. Say it. Mississippi—it's easy." The subject gingerly says it.

Then suddenly exclaim, "Close your mouth! Close it tight, tight, tighter! Clench up that jaw!" Make passes over and about his locked jaw, as you rapidly suggest, "Your jaw is locked tight shut, you cannot open it! Try hard to open that jaw! You cannot do it! It is tight shut!"

The subject vainly tries, and you carry right on. "In fact you can't speak a single word. Now try hard to speak . . . you cannot! You cannot speak a single word try as hard as you will! Try! Try hard! Your mouth is relaxed now. You can open your mouth, but you cannot utter a single sound. Go ahead and open your mouth." The subject does so, but he cannot speak, and you follow right on through, "In fact, you cannot remember your own name. You have completely forgotten your name. You can speak now. Say 'Hello' to me." The subject says "Hello," and you continue, "You can speak now, but you cannot say your own name. You have forgotten it!" **Place the forefinger of your right hand directly in the center of the subject's forehead and press in,** continue, "You cannot remember your own name, but you can speak now. What is your name? Try hard to remember it. Try hard! You have completely forgotten your own name!"

The subject will develop sort of a blank look on his face; suddenly realizing that he has, indeed, completely lost memory of his own name. You can take your finger away from the subject's head now, and ask him quizzically, "Just what is your name? All right, I will tell you." Give him some funny sounding name like Oswalt Flopper for instance, and repeat over and over, "Your name is Oswalt Flopper! Your name is Oswalt Flopper! What is your name? It is Oswalt Flopper! Tell me your name! It is Oswalt Flopper! Tell me your name! Tell me your name! It is Oswalt Flopper!"

The subject will suddenly blurt out that his name is Oswalt Flopper! Immediately clap your hands beside him, and say, "All right. It's all gone. You can remember your real name now perfectly. What is your real name?" And the subject gives it. You then thank him and ask him to return to his seat.

You will notice here in this test the use of what is called the "confusion technique." Each suggestion is heaped upon the subject in rapid succession. Each test leads directly one from the other with scarcely a pause between each. Your manner is aggressive, and the subject is given little time to think as you forcefully pile suggestion upon suggestion.

Heavy Water — Shaky Pouring — Drunk on a Glass of Water Test

We come now to a very humorous experiment. Bring another person forward. **Be certain that you use for this test a subject that you are positive will respond to your suggestions.** If possible use one that you have not previously experimented with, but the nature of this test is such that you can repeat a subject if necessary. Have him sit in a chair near the center of the stage as you gaze in his eyes, and suggest that he will respond to every suggestion presented strongly and positively. When his eyes take on that intense fascinated look, tell him to go over to the side of the stage and lift up a glass and pitcher of water which rests on the table there (See Fig. 50). This he does. Tell him then to set them again on the table, and to retain his grip tightly on them, and to concentrate on your suggestions, as you say, "Now that glass and pitcher of water are becoming very heavy. So very heavy that they are stuck to the table. You cannot lift them. Try hard to lift them, but you cannot!" The subject tries hard to raise the objects but is unable to do so.

FIG. 50

While he is tugging, you approach him and suggest, "All right now. You can lift the pitcher and the glass easily. Lift them right up now, and pour the water from the pitcher into the glass." The subject responds, and you continue, "See, already your hands are beginning to shake . . . your hands are getting nervous. You are shaking so much that the water is spilling about every place. You cannot control that shaking!" As you give these suggestions get in close beside your subject, and make your own motions jerky and nervous—shaking your hands spasmodically. Give your suggestions in a short jerky manner; make your voice quite loud. Your subject will follow right along with you; his hands will begin to shake, and he will soon be spilling water every which way. Your suggestions seemingly are not directed so much at him as the objects that he is handling, and sort of gently scold him as you hammer them home, as, "Why are you so nervous? Look your hands are shaking all over the place. Why can't you hold them still? You're spilling water all over yourself. What makes you so nervous anyway?"

After the subject has spilled the water about good and plenty, quiet him with, "All right now. You're all calm now. Calm now. Take the pitcher and fill the glass with water. That's it. Isn't it easy now? Take the glass of water right back to your chair, and have a seat."

Standing now in front of the subject, a bit to his right side so that the audience can plainly see all that happens, you tell him to take a sip of the water, and ask him how it tastes? Then catch his eye firmly, and suggest forcefully,

"That water no longer tastes good. It is old and stagnant. It is old vile, putrid, sewer water ... the kind with the green scum on top! It reeks with an awful, vile smell. How you hate it! Take a sip of that vile, putrid, scummy water. Just a little sip, cause it will make you feel sick ... and spit it out right away!" Force your subject to take a sip of it, and as he drinks it, follow right on through with your suggestions, "How vile it tastes! Spit it out! Spit it out!" The subject will wrinkle up his nose, go through a wonderful pantomime of disgust, and end up by violently spitting out the water, much to the delight of the audience.

Immediately catch his eye again, and tell him, "All

right now, that bad taste is all gone. It's all gone. The taste is now all sweet and good, in fact, you are not holding a glass of water now at all—it is a glass of gin! Good, sweet, powerful gin. And how you are going to like it, but be very careful of it, it is mighty strong and will make you drunk. But my, how you will like it! Take a sip of that gin." The subject sips, and you say, "That's enough. Say, doesn't that taste good, and how warm it glows as it passes down your throat. Here have some more. Drink some more. Say, you're begininng to get drunk. How warm and happy you feel. Drink some more. Say, everything is beginning to seem funny. You want to laugh, to giggle. Go ahead, laugh and giggle." The subject will soon grin from ear to ear and giggle foolishly, and you continue, "Say, you are drunk! I bet you cannot even stand up from that chair. You're so drunk. So drunk. Try and get up from that chair." The subject tries, but flops back unable to get out of it, and you continue, "Here I'll help you, but look how unsteady you are on your feet. You're drunk! Now that you're on your feet, see if you can stand alone." The subject wobbles about drunkenly and you continue, "Say, you are unstable on your legs; your knees must feel like rubber. Try and walk a straight line, follow me. Come now, say, you're staggering all over the place. You are drunk. You sure are drunk!"

As you give these suggestions to induce drunkenness, emphasize your suggestions by putting a sort of drunken "sing-song" in your voice, and let yourself sort of stagger about along with the subject as you help him up out of the chair and have him follow you about the stage. **It is important that you dramatize all suggestions of this sort.** Then lead him from one end of the stage to the other, having him follow you staggeringly, finally end up near the center of the stage.

You point to an imaginary spot in the air, as you say, "Look up there. See that bright light . . . way out there? See it! Look at it!" The subject stares, and you continue, "Say, that light is beginning to get larger. It's getting closer to us!" Gesture with your hands as though it were passing through the air and coming up right onto the stage, then point to the floor, at the subject's feet, as you say, "Here it is on the floor. Look it isn't a light at all—it's a **mouse!** It's running all about!" Make your suggestion with mounting excitement, "It's a mouse, and it's running up your leg! Get it out! Get it out!" Suddenly bend over, move your finger rapidly in zigzag, low to the stage, as though you were following the running course of the mouse, and plunge your right hand up the cuff of his pants leg, as you say excitedly, "Get it out! Get it out!"

The subject will jump about, shaking his leg trying to rid himself of the imaginary mouse. You bring a chair forward, tell him to get up on it to get away from the mouse. And when the action is at its pitch, suddenly clap your hands and say, "All right. It's all gone! It's all gone!" You are safe in thus ending this experiment rapidly, as basically deep trance has not been induced. The subject will usually be quite confused after this experiment, will shake his head and be generally bewildered. You thank him, and he returns to his seat.

You have observed in this experiment a very interesting type of hypnotic phenomenon, for you have produced a hallucination in the waking stage. Actually, there is no real difference in the mental condition of the subject influenced in his waking state than under hypnosis except in the matter of degree of responsiveness, and as long as your waking suggestions are accepted and acted upon, they are every bit as effective as if they were presented under complete hypnosis.

We are now rapidly approaching the type of phenomenon generally classed as hypnotic, so turn to the audience and address them, "Thus far you have witnessed demonstrations in suggestion in what is called the wakeful state of mind. Let us now experiment with the actual induction of hypnotism. Who would like to volunteer to be the first subject?"

Inducing the Hypnotic Trance

Point to someone in the committee that you feel would respond best to the test; if you wish, choose a subject, who, while responsive, has been somewhat sluggish in reacting to waking tests. In every committee you are bound to note such persons, and this is a good chance to put one to work. Bring the subject forward and have him sit in a chair, center stage, with his right side toward the spectators; you take a position in front of the subject ready to hypnotize. Now, first, ask the subject a few questions.

"Have you ever been hypnotized? Are you perfectly willing to be hypnotized?" Get his answers and then explain, "Now, Hypnotism is a condition very closely resembling sleep. The major difference is this, however. If I were to approach you while you slept and were to talk to you, you would be disturbed and might wake up. Right? However, when you are hypnotized, I can talk to you all that time and you will not be disturbed, but will go right on sleeping. You see your condition in hypnosis is almost exactly the same as when a person walks in their sleep. See what I mean?"

Turn to the committee and say, "Now everyone observe very closely this experiment, for just as soon as we are through, we will all try Hypnotism together." Here you again set pre-hypnotic suggestions that will assist you in later hypnotizing them all.

Directly facing your subject, bend towards him slightly (See Fig. 25) and hypnotize him by the progressive method. However, on the stage you can usually condense it, and proceed very rapidly, as you say, "Look me directly in the eye, the right one. Let your gaze remain fixed and fastened there. Your eyes are becoming riveted to mine, and already your eyelids are beginning to get heavy. Your eyes are beginning to burn. How you want to close them. But you cannot close them yet, for they are fastened intently upon my eye. But now I will count slowly from one to ten, and with every count your eyes will become heavier and heavier, until by the time I reach ten, or before, you will close shut those tired eyes. Ready, One—two. Those eyes are so tired. So tired. Close those tired eyes. Three—four. Close those tired eyelids. Get that pleasant relief. Five—Six—Seven. That's it, close those tired eyes. How good it does feel to close those tired eyes. Close them tight. Tight. Eight. Eyes all closed. Nine—Ten. Now those eyes are becoming stuck tightly together." Here you lean forward and make contact passes over his eyes, rubbing outward from the root of the nose toward the temples, and suggest, "Your eyes are stuck so tightly together that they simply will not open. See how they stick!" The subject tries in vain to open his eyes, and you follow right on, "All right, forget all about your eyes now, and go sound to sleep. Go deep asleep. Deep, deep asleep." Step to the rear of your subject, stroke his forehead a few times, and then stroke the back of his head from the crown down to the nape of the neck (See Fig. 51), as you continue to suggest, "You are going down deep, deep asleep. Go sound to sleep!"

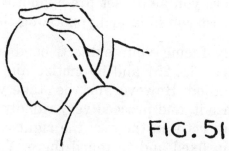

FIG. 51

Watch the subject's breathing, and as it deepens, suggest, "Your breaths are coming in deeper and deeper. Deep and free, and every breath you take is sending you down deeper and deeper to sleep." Then place your left hand on his left shoulder and press downward firmly, so that his body tends to slump down in his chair. At the same time, with your right hand tilt his head forward on his chest (See Fig. 52), as you continue, "Everything is going so far, far away. You are deep, deep asleep." Then step to the front of your subject, and as you suggest that every muscle in his entire body is relaxed and asleep, pick up one of his hands and let it drop limply to his side. Let his other hand drop likewise. Put your hand on the back of the subject's neck and push his head down so that it rests on his knees (See Fig. 53).

Again pick up his arm and let drop rag-like to his side. Take hold of both arms and flop them about. They behave just like they were on loose strings. This always causes a rise from the audience, so you address them, "You will note that perfect relaxation. And right here you are observing one of the most important aspects of the hypnotic trance itself—the complete relaxation it can produce. And yet, a mere suggestion and that relaxation can change instantly to catalepsy."

FIG. 52

FIG. 53

Pick up the subject's right hand and stretch it out straight from his shoulder as you suggest, "Your arm and hand are becoming stiff, **Stiff!** Hold it out straight and stiff." You can feel the muscles of the arm contract, then let go of the hand, and the arm remains outstretched in the air, as you suggest, "That arm is becoming so stiff and rigid that you simply cannot bend it no matter how hard you try!" The subject tries to bend it, but the arm resists all of his efforts and remains stiff. Then pick up his left arm and hold it outstretched also, and say loudly, **"Stiff!"** That arm, too, becomes stiff and rigid. Both of the subject's arms are now outstretched in the air (See Fig. 54), as you again speak to the audience, "Now watch the instant return to relaxation."

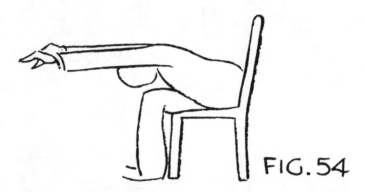

FIG. 54

Again address the subject, "The moment I reach the count of three your arms will instantly relax and fall limply to your sides, and the moment they hit your sides they will send you down deeper and deeper into the very deepest trance. All ready, when I reach the count of three, your arms will instantly relax and fall like rags to your sides." Gently touch the sides of his thighs as you give these suggestions, then count slowly, "One—two—three." Instantly the arms collapse and drop dead-like to the subject's sides. Again flop them about illustrating their complete relaxation, then address the audience, "The subject could sleep thus in the hypnotic trance for a number of hours, but time passes rapidly, so let's remove the state at once. Now, the one thing most people seem to feel is dangerous about hypnotism is the removal of the trance, but actually there is no danger whatsoever if it is handled correctly. So note how gently and easily the subject awakens."

Now address the subject, "You have been having a most pleasant sleep and it has done you a great deal of good, but now the time is coming to awaken. So get ready to wake up. I will count slowly from one to five —with every count you will gradually awaken, and by the time I reach five be wide, wide awake. All ready. One—two—three—four—five. That's it. Stretch yourself. Didn't that feel good. Thank you, and now you may return to your seat."

In performing on the stage always hypnotize as rapidly as you can, as a long drawn-out technique of sleep inducing is scarcely highly entertaining to the audience. Fortunately, the stage situation makes it possible to often hypnotize in a matter of seconds. Some subjects will go to sleep almost instantly the moment they close their eyes, and you have but to command, **"Sleep,"** and proceed directly into the arm catalepsy test. **This rapidity of trance induction is one of the marvels that thrills the audience.**

Seventh Group Experiment — Mass Hypnotism

Face your committee and say, "All right everyone, let's all try the experiment together. After all, you came on this stage for the expressed purpose of being hypnotized, so here is your chance to enter this very interesting state. So everyone give it your undivided attention and concentrate to the utmost, and I will also do my very best to help you."

"All ready, seat yourselves back comfortably in your chairs, place your feet flat on the floor, and let your hands rest in your lap. That's right, let one hand rest on each knee, so that your fingers will not touch. Now each of you direct your gaze directly towards me, and all together, when I say inhale, inhale a deep breath. Hold it, and then exhale as I direct. Everyone now, **inhale.**" With your hands outstretched above your head move them downward toward your sides as you inhale, and upward as you exhale (See Fig. 55), continue, "Hold it. Hold it, now, exhale slowly. Good. Now one last time. Inhale, hold it, and exhale.

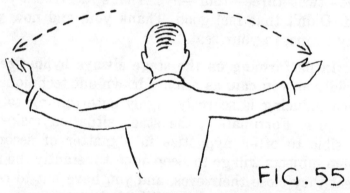

FIG. 55

"How nice and relaxed that makes you feel, and as you look directly at me, all ready you begin to feel a calmness creeping over you, a pleasant sensation of warmth all about you, and your eyes begin to feel heavy and tired. They want to close. All right, I will count slowly from one to ten, and with every count they will slowly close, so by the time I reach ten or before, close your eyelids right down tight and shut out the light. Ready. One—two—three—four—eyes closing all down tight. Five—six—seven. Close those tired eyes and let them rest. Eight—nine—ten. Eyes all closed together."

Look over the entire committee; all eyes should be closed. If any are not, point to that person and request him to close his eyes, then continue, "It feels so good to close those tired eyes. So good, and they are so tightly closed that they are getting all stuck together. Those eyes are stuck, they won't open. See how they stick."

In working with the entire committee, don't make an issue of this, but rather continue rapidly on, "Forget all about your eyes now and go to sleep. Go sound to sleep. Sleep. Sleepy sleep. Going down deep, deep asleep. Go sound to sleep."

By now many subjects will be nodding and breathing deeply, so starting at the left end of the semi-circle go to each in turn, rapidly make a few contact passes over their foreheads from the root of the nose out towards the temples, and suggest directly into the ear of each, "That's right. You are concentrating splendidly. Go sound to sleep now. Nothing will bother you. Just go sound, sound to sleep." Then push their head forward a bit so it falls relaxed on their chest, and repeat the process with the next subject on through the entire group. Work rapidly, then return to stage center and suggest, "Nothing will bother you at all. You are all sleeping pleasantly and deeply. Go deeper and deeper to sleep. You are breathing deep and free, deep and free, and every breath you take is sending you on down deeper and deeper to sleep. Go deep, deep asleep. Sound asleep."

Look over your subjects carefully now, for here is your chance to diplomatically get rid of those persons you do not wish to keep on the stage. So, if any sub-

jects are obviously deliberately not responding or are "cutting up," quietly approach them, and whisper, "Thank you very much for volunteering, but will you quietly leave the stage now. Walk down very quietly please so as not to disturb any of the sleeping subjects. **Be firm about this and rid yourself of all of your undesirable material at this time.** There is important psychology at work here: the words are naturally picked up by the responsive subjects and it unconsciously flatters them to know that they are performing correctly, and that you keep them while sending down others, and it naturally empties the stage of unresponsive persons in a very logical manner at a time when you obviously would not wish to retain any wakeful persons who might possibly disturb the sleeping subjects. Continue on with your suggestions.

Group Hand Raising Test

"Now, in a moment you will begin to feel a sort of tingling sensation coming into your fingertips. It will be a very pleasant tingle, and you can feel it passing up your arms. It makes your hands restless in your lap. Your hands are getting lighter and lighter; they are beginning to raise up from your laps. Your hands are raising up. Hands raising right up from your lap. Raise your hands up. Raise them up! All hands coming up. UP! Hold them outstretched straight out from the shoulders. That's it. All hands outstretched directly out from your shoulders."

Observe your committee closely. Hands will begin to slowly raise up from the laps of subjects all along the semi-circle. Some will respond more rapidly than others; as long as you have a good showing you need not bother to take the time to make every subject respond. But get a good two-thirds of them up in the air (See Fig. 56).

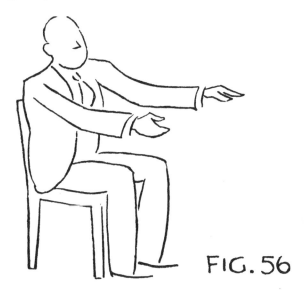

FIG. 56

Spot the five subjects who raised their hands up first. Walk over to the one nearest you, touch him lightly on the head, and command, "Rise up out of your chair and walk!" Take him by the hand and get him started. As soon as he is on his feet and walking, pass on to each of the remaining spotted subjects and repeat the test. The effect of the five subjects slowly walking across the stage, Zombie fashion, with their arms stretched out in front of them, is weird and startling.

Keep your eye on the subjects so that none of them get too close to the edge of the stage. Then go to each in turn, and say sharply, **"Stop!** Every muscle of your body is frozen in that position. You cannot move!" The subjects stand like statues in whatever position they happened to be when you gave the command.

Next go back to the seated group, rapidly walk to

each, touch him on the hand and say, "Follow every suggestion that I give you." This serves to focus their attention strongly on you as you suggest, "There are two things I want you to remember. When I reach the count of five you will be wide awake and feeling fine. **But,** you will find that you cannot lower your arms no matter how hard you try, until I snap my fingers by your ear . . . then and then only will your arms lower. Remember, when I reach the count of five you will be wide awake, but you will be unable to lower your arms until I snap my fingers by your ear. And secondly, remember, the moment I point my finger directly at your forehead, you will go instantly to sleep no matter what you may be doing. Remember, the moment I point my finger at your forehead you will go instantly asleep no matter what you may be doing. All ready now, get ready to wake up with your arms frozen out straight in front of you. One—two—three—four—**five!**"

The subjects awake in various stages of bewilderment at finding themselves unable to lower their arms. The five standing subjects also awake with their arms "frozen." **Here is your perfect chance to spot the somnambulistic subjects you wish to use in the advanced tests shortly to climax your show.** If a subject responds forcefully to this post-hypnotic suggestion, then you know he is one of those you will use . . . **so spot them well.**

When this test of the "frozen arms" has proceeded long enough to prove its full effect, rapidly release each person by snapping your fingers beside his ear. Request the standing subjects to return to their seats, and you are ready for the next test.

The Cigarette Test

Turn and directly address the audience, "Amazing as some of these experiments seem upon the stage, the real wonders of Hypnotism come from its clinical value. For example, in the way, it can correct such habits as smoking and drinking. Let me illustrate its power by removing the cigarette habit." Turn towards the subjects, and ask, "Who among you smoke cigarettes?"

Select someone who smokes, who, from the previous test, you know to be a responsive subject, and have him step forward and take a seat center stage. Next conduct a little quiz, asking him how long he has smoked, how many cigarettes he smokes each day, if by way of an experiment he would be willing to overcome the habit, etc. Finally have him light a cigarette and ask him how it tastes. He'll say "Fine," or smile in satisfaction. Then request him to look directly into your eyes, to think of himself floating far, far away, down deep into the hypnotic sleep ... and then, **Point your finger directly at his forehead.** Instantly the posthypnotic suggestion you previously gave goes into action, and he drops over in his chair, sound asleep.

Then suggest, "Now we are together going to overcome a habit that you have had for a long time—the habit of smoking. You will find that the next time you smoke, that you will no longer care for the cigarette. It will taste dry and parched in your mouth. It will taste like old soggy straw. You won't care for them anymore. In fact you hate cigarettes; they taste so bad. They make your mouth all dry and parched. You will throw them away in disgust. And they make you choke and cough. Even the smoke makes you choke and cough. You hate even the smell of the smoke."

As you give the above suggestions commenting on the smoke, **hold the smoking cigarette directly under the subject's nose,** and continue to suggest, "You hate even the smoke. You want to get away from it. Turn your head away from that smoke." Almost immediately the subject will cough and sneeze, a disgusted curl comes on his lips, and he will turn his head away from the smoking cigarette. This is your cue to climax your suggestion with, "All right now, when I say 'Three' you will open your eyes, but you will find that you hate cigarettes, and will throw it away in disgust. One—two—three—Open your eyes and try the cigarette."

You will note that you have not directly awakened the subject, but merely suggested that he open his eyes. In most cases the test would work equally well post-hypnotically, but for the purpose of this stage demonstration let him remain in a sort of half trance to arouse himself as he will. Proceed right on.

"Here, try the cigarette." Force it between the subject's lips, and say, "Take a good puff of it. How you hate that cigarette. Throw it away in disgust!" The subject will take a drag, cough, sputter, and throw the cigarette from him with vengeance.

You then turn and address the audience, "You see here an example of how a habit can be rapidly removed through hypnosis. This subject has admitted that he has smoked cigarettes for a number of years, and yet, in less than two minutes time, he now finds himself utterly unable to smoke. Let us try the test with a different brand of cigarettes. Someone lend me a cigarette, please." Someone obliges.

You hand the cigarette to the subject, place it to his lips and light it for him, as you say, "You will find this one will taste ten times as bad as the other one. It will actually make you feel sick. Oh, how you hate cigarettes!" The subject will again cough, much to the amusement of the spectators, and will throw the cigarette far from him, and you say, "Let's bring the old, good taste back again, shall we? Look me in the eyes. Your eyes are growing heavy all ready . . . close them and go to sleep. Go to sleep!" Your subject already in a half trance will respond immediately. You carry on with the suggestion.

"In a moment, I will count from one to five, at the count of five you will be wide awake and feeling fine. And you will find that cigarettes taste all good and sweet again, just as they always have. You will enjoy your smoking thoroughly. All ready now, I will count from one to five, and at the count of five you will be wide awake, and will enjoy smoking just like you always have. One—two—three—four—five." The subject awakes, you offer him a cigarette which he now smokes with obvious enjoyment.

Since he has proved himself a good subject, leave him sitting right where he is for the next test, and point to six or seven other subjects in the committee. Use the subjects you have previously spotted as being responsive to the post-hypnotic suggestion of having their "arms frozen." Ask them to move their chairs forward and form a line near the center of the stage, and take a seat (See Fig. 57).

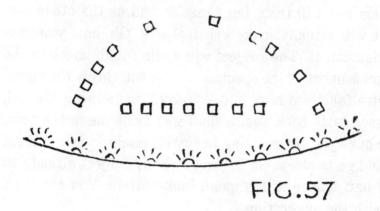

FIG.57

Hypnotizing from the Audience

You then address the audience, "I will now show you a type of hypnotic demonstration that is very rarely performed . . . hypnotizing a group of persons, all at the same time, from the rear of the audience itself." Then to your subjects explain, "I am going right down into the audience, and from there attempt to hypnotize you. So pay very close attention to me, and concentrate with all of your ability."

And to the audience again, say, "And you in the audience can assist me a great deal in this difficult experiment, if you, too, will hold in your minds the idea of these subjects, here on the stage, going down deep into the hypnotic trance."

Then, just before you leave the stage, turn towards the committee, and add, "Now primarily I am going to concentrate on these subjects here in the front row, but if there are others in the back group who wish to also participate in the experiment, feel free to do so, and concentrate right along with them. All right everyone, with back in your chairs, feet together, hands in your lap, and all ready for the experiment of hypnotizing from the rear of the audience."

Your conditions for this dramatic test are all pretty well set before you even start. The row of eight subjects in front represent your most responsive material from the group, so are almost certain to go easily into hypnosis. Some of the remaining committee members also will be passable subjects, so you have paved the way for them likewise to enter the trance if they choose to follow. Frequently many do, and you can then bring them forward and add to the front group for inclusion in the climactic tests yet to come. Those persons that do not respond are seated well back on the stage anwaw, and are not bothersome. Just let them sit there as observers, and their merriment at the subjects' reactions will only add to the general enjoyment of the audience. Go down into the audience, stand on an aisle seat in their midst, and call out to your subjects to look directly at you in the audience.

You suggest, "As you look out here at me, and concentrate your attention towards my eyes, already you begin to feel yourself getting sleepy, and the hypnotic trance is coming over you. Your eyes are getting heavy, and the lids want to close. Close those tired, tired eyes." Point your right forefinger out towards the subjects **and sweep it in an arc so it covers each of them.** Thanks to your previous post-hypnotic suggestion, they will almost at once close their eyes and start to nod. You will amaze even yourself at how rapidly they will respond at this point in your show, as you continue, "You are going to sleep. Deep, deep asleep. Go sound asleep, etc." As you follow on with the "sleep formula" walk back up on the stage to the rear of the subject on the right end of the front group. Stroke his forehead a few times, press on his shoulders so he slumps in his chair, and push his hands off his lap so that they dangle limply at his sides, as you continue to suggest, "Nothing will bother you in the least. You are sleeping deep. Keep going deep, deeper to sleep. Sound asleep."

Then go to the subject sleeping beside him, and repeat the process, Just before you pass on to the next subject in the row push the heads of the first and second subject together so that they support each other (See Fig. 58). This is a very whimsical bit of business.

FIG. 58

The Revolving Arms Test

When all of the front row of subjects are sleeping peacefully, look around your back group, and if any others in the committee are asleep, go to them and push their heads down into their laps, as you instruct them to go on sleeping down deeper and deeper.

Then go back to the first subject in the front row, lift up his hands, turn them parallel to each other, and start them rotating rapidly around each other, as you say to him, "Keep those hands revolving. They will not stop. The more you try to stop them, the faster they go. Try and stop them. You cannot. They are revolving faster and faster." Work rapidly down the row until every one of the subjects is rapidly revolving their arms around each other (See Fig. 59).

FIG. 59

Then say to the group, "Your hands are revolving around faster and faster. You cannot stop them. But when I say 'Three' they will instantly stop, and freeze dead in the air, and you will find you cannot move them try as hard as you will. When I say three they will instantly stop and freeze dead still in the air. One —two—**Three!**"

Instantly, the revolving arms freeze dead still in the air. The subjects can't move them try as hard as they will. Then suggest, "When I say 'Go', around and around your hands will revolve again." Suddenly shout, **"Go!"** Immediately the hands commence to revolve in frenzy, as you suggest, "Around and around they go, faster and faster!"

While the arms are revolving at a pitch, step quietly behind the first subject of the row, make a few passes without contact in front of his face, and quietly suggest directly into his ear, "It's all going away. You are going back to sleep. Your arms are dropping to your lap. You are going fast, fast to sleep."

The visible transformation of moods that flit across the subject's face as he slips from violent motion into peaceful slumber is fascinating to behold. Push his hands off his lap so that they dangle at his sides, and leave him sleeping as you pass from one subject to the next, leaving each sleeping in turn, until the entire row of subjects are all again sleeping soundly.

The Canary Bird Test

Then address the group, "At the count of three you will all open your eyes, and you will see in your left hand the cutest little canary bird you ever saw. And you will love this little bird, and have just a wonderful time playing with it.

"All ready now, get ready to play with the little bird. Sit back in your chairs, and hold out your left hands so you can look at the little bird." The subjects will respond, adjusting themselves in their chairs and holding out their left hands cup-like, as you repeat the suggestions, "Remember, at the count of three you will open your eyes and look directly at the palm of your left hand, and in it you will see the cutest, little, yellow canary bird you ever saw. And as you look at it, and play with it, it will send you down deeper and deeper to sleep all the time. Get ready now to look at that little yellow bird in your left hand. One—two—**Three.**"

The subjects open their eyes, stare at the palm of their left hand as you continue, "Pat that little bird now. Isn't it cute? Hold it gently. Let it hop onto your finger if it wants to." The subjects will begin going through a variety of pantomimes of patting and playing with the little bird in their hand.

Advance to one of the subjects who is responding well, place your finger in his left palm, and wave it in the air, as you say, "There goes the little bird flying about. Catch it! Catch it!" The subject will grab air trying to get it. Then tell him to chase it, and he will leave his seat, chasing about the stage after it.

Make the "little bird" fly about from the hands of a few other subjects until you have plenty of action on the stage. **Keep a careful eye on the subjects, as they move about the stage, to make sure they don't get too near the footlights where they might fall off.**

Then go to each subject who is trying to catch the imaginary bird, and say, "Here it is, here is the little bird," as you pretend to catch and hand it to him, and add, "Hold it gently, but don't let it get away." The subject will at once cup it in his hands carefully, and you suggest, "Take it and go back to your seat." When all of the subjects are again in their seats, patting the "bird," step behind the subject seated at the end of the row, make a few passes in front of his face and suggest, "You are getting sleepy again. The little bird is all gone now. Forget all about the little bird and go sound, sound to sleep." As the subject slumps over in the trance, whisper directly into his ear so that only he can hear the post-hypnotic suggestion you previously gave, "Remember, the moment I point my finger at your forehead you will go instantly asleep."

Go to each of the subjects in turn and place them again in the trance, **quietly repeating to each the important post-hypnotic suggestion, "Remember, the moment I point my finger at your forehead you will go** instantly asleep." The audience has no awareness of this repeated post-hypnotic suggestion. To them it seems that you are merely returning the subjects to the trance. Save your subject who is showing the most reaction to the "little canary" to the last, and when all of the others are sleeping peacefully with the exception of him, walk over by his side and say, "You know that I am also a Magician, so let me show you my famous vanishing canary bird trick. Hold the little bird perched right up on your finger. That's it, fine. Now watch very closely, for I am going to count slowly from one to three, and at the count of three that canary bird will disappear right before your very eyes, right while it's perched on your very finger. Don't let me fool you, so watch very, very closely. Ready. One—two—and **three**—the bird is **gone!**" The subject will stare, and the stark amazement written all over his face is a delight to the audience.

Quickly return the subject to deep sleep, and address the entire group, "You are all sleeping soundly now, but in a moment you will all be wide, wide awake and feel just fine and good all over. I will count slowly from one to five, and at the count of five, you will be wide, wide awake, just a little bewildered and confused at finding that you have slept so long. Ready. One—two—three—four—five. Wide, wide awake and feeling all fine."

The subjects awaken, rubbing their eyes, stretching, generally confused, much to the amusement of everyone.

The Instantaneous Hypnotism Test

Then turn and directly speak to the audience, "You are now aboüt to witness what has been called the fastest demonstration of Hypnotism on the stage to-day—Instantaneous Hypnosis."

Go to one of the subjects in the row, have him stand up and move about. Ask him if he is sure that he is wide awake and feels perfectly normal. When he has said, "Yes," have him move his chair a little forward from the group and take his seat. **Then, suddenly turn, point your finger directly at his forehead, and shout, "Sleep!"** Instantly the subject drops over in a trance.

Then suggest to the subject, "When you wake up again at the count of five you will feel perfectly normal in all ways, but you will find that you are stuck, glued to the seat of your chair. You cannot get out of it. Pull as hard as you will you cannot get free from that chair until I clap my hands beside your ear, then you will come instantly free! All ready, at the count of five you will be again wide, wide awake. One—two—three—four—five." The subject awakens, you ask him to try and rise up from the chair, but he is stuck tight. He tugs and tugs, but cannot get free. Right while he is in the middle of a violent tug, suddenly clap your hands, and he will bound up from his seat with a rush. Thank him, and have him return his chair to the row and be seated.

Then quietly walk past the row of subjects, turn suddenly on a subject, catch his eye, point your finger directly at his forehead, and shout, **"Sleep!"** Instantly he goes to sleep. Hypnotize thus two others. The way those subjects, one moment wide awake, suddenly take a little gasp and slump over in unconsciousness is positively uncanny. This test looks like a modern miracle.

The Amnesia Test

Three subjects are now deeply entranced as you address the audience, "You have all heard tales of missing persons, who show up strangely in different cities, and yet when questioned by the police they seem utterly unable to remember their names, where they are from, or anything about themselves. Such persons are called amnesia victims, amnesia being a peculiar mental condition characterized by loss of memory. Now this state of amnesia can be experimentally demonstrated through hypnosis, let us attempt such an experiment." Turn towards your three sleeping subjects, and say, "In a moment I am going to awaken you, and when you wake up a strange thing will have happened. You will feel fine in every way and perfectly normal, **but** you will find that you cannot remember your own names try as hard as you will. Not only will you be unable to remember your own names, but you won't have the slightest idea of where you are, how you got here, or anything about yourselves. Your minds will be a complete blank. You won't remember your own names, where you are, or anything about yourselves ... until I snap my fingers beside your ear, then everything will come back to you instantly. Remember now, after you awaken you will feel fine in every way, but you will not be able to remember your own names, who you are, or anything about yourselves ... until I snap my fingers beside your ear, then everything will come back to you in a flash. Ready now. At the count of five you will be wide awake. One—two—three—four—five."

The subjects awaken with a sort of blank look on their faces. You bring one of them forward to the front of the stage and ask a few questions, as, "How do you feel?" The subject answers, "Fine." "Would you like to tell the audience who you are?" The subject looks blank and appears uncomfortable. "Well, what is your name?" No response. "Come, tell us your name. Try hard to remember. Well, if you can't remember your name, tell us where you are?" The subject thinks hard and shakes his head. "Can't you recall even where you are or anything about yourself? Try hard and remember." The subject shakes his head in bewilderment. "All right now, keep thinking hard and observe what happens." You suddenly snap your fingers beside his ear. Instantly the blank look vanishes from his face, and the subject smiles relieved as you again ask, "Can you tell us your name now?" The subject answers, "Of course," and gives his name. You thank him and he resumes his seat.

Call the second subject forward, let us say you use a girl this time for variety, and you repeat the test— she being totally unable to give her name or tell anything about herself until you snap your fingers by her ear. It is extremely interesting to observe the many variety of responses the subjects will go through as they react to such an experience. Some will tend to get panicky and even cry, while others will take it all with a stoic calmness. When the test is complete, thank the young lady, gesture her to her seat, and explain to the audience, "You have seen here some examples of experimentally produced amnesia. In normal life the amnesia is usually produced through a mental conflict from which the person tries to hide by retreating into this condition. Basically, there is very little difference between that spontaneously induced amnesia and that here produced through hypnotism. Let us now test this last subject.

Again you proceed with the test, asking the subject various questions about himself that he seems utterly unable to answer, and worrying him some as you ask him what he intends to do to get out of his predicament. Then to climax the experiment you borrow a small hand mirror, and hold it up directly in front of the subject's face, as you ask,

"Whom do you see in the mirror?" The subject usually says, "A face." "Is it a nice face?" you question, "Do you like it?" The subject shakes his head. "All right now, watch that face closely and see what happens." Suddenly snap your fingers; the subject starts, smiles, and sheepishly admits that it's his face he sees in the mirror. Thank all of the subjects, and have them return with their chairs back to the row.

The Motion Picture Test

We come now to one of the most striking experiments you can possibly perform, a test that literally convulses the audience.

Stand in front of your row of subjects, ask them to look at you, and hypnotize them very quickly with a few suggestions of sleep, while at the same time pointing your forefinger directly towards them, as you sweep it slowly from one end of the line to the other. When the group are sleeping soundly, go rapidly to each and push them farther down in their chair, as you repeat in the ear of each, "Sleep, sleep deep. Sound asleep." Then address the whole group as a body.

"In a moment you will all open your eyes, and you will see before you a motion picture screen, and on it will be a very exciting western melodrama. You are going to have a wonderful time watching this picture. You will see the hero and the heroine. You will see the villain and the comedian, and you will just have a wonderful time watching this picture unreel before your eyes.

"Get ready, everybody, to watch this picture. Sit back, up straight in your chairs, and at the count of three open your eyes and watch the movie. All ready, one—two—**three.** Open your eyes and watch the picture."

The subjects all open their eyes, and staring out excitedly in front of them lean forward in their chairs, as you suggest,

"Now the picture is getting very exciting. You're having a wonderful time. And here comes the comedian. Say, isn't that fellow funny. You never saw anyone so funny before, you just want to laugh and laugh. Go ahead, laugh and laugh."

Give your suggestions with all of the enthusiasm of a sports announcer, and as you narrate the occurrences of the imaginary drama interpret it in your voice. When you say, laugh, **really laugh.** And how those subjects will respond. They will literally convulse with laughter, and you can build that laughter up to a higher and higher pitch. And right when it's at its peak, suddenly change your mood, and suggest, "It's not funny any more, the story is getting sad. The poor mother is out in the snow freezing to death, and her children are in the little log cabin starving to death. Oh, you feel so sad. You've never felt so sad in your entire life."

The transformation is astonishing as those subjects immediately shift from gales of laughter to sadness, and some of them even begin to cry. Then suggest, "Look, everything is all right, and it's getting funny again. You want to laugh at it. Laugh! Go ahead and laugh!"

Get all of the subjects laughing once more, then step behind each in turn and send him down to sleep again, with, "Alright, the picture is fading away now. It is all gone. You are going down sound, sound to sleep. Go to sleep."

And what of the subjects in the back group near the rear of the stage? The ones of these that respond you can bring forward and include in the tests along with the subjects in the front row at any time that conveniently fits in with your routine. The entire group of subjects now asleep, you thank the rest of the committee seated in the rear semi-circle and ask them to return quietly to their seats in the audience. **Send down all persons from the stage who are not sleeping at this point,** and you are ready to perform your concluding test.

The Post-Hypnotic Climax

For this experiment give your suggestions very forcefully and deliberately.

You say, "You have all had a good, long sleep on the stage, and in just a moment I am going to awaken you. And when you awake you will all feel fine and refreshed, but you will find that you cannot leave the stage because your left foot is stuck to the floor. And pull and tug as hard as you will, you will not be able to free your left foot . . . until I snap my fingers by your ear . . . then your left foot will come free, but your right foot will get stuck to the stage.

"All right, I will now count slowly from one to five. With every count you will gradually wake up, and by the time I reach five be wide, wide awake . . . BUT you will find you cannot leave the stage because your left foot will be glued, stuck to the floor . . . and it will not come free until I snap my fingers by your ear when your left foot will come free, but your right will then get stuck. When I snap my fingers again, your right foot will then come free, but your left foot will get stuck to the floor all over again. And so it will go back and forth . . . first one foot stuck to the floor, and then the other everytime I snap my fingers . . . until I clap my hands loudly beside you, and say it's all gone.

"All ready now. I will count from one to five, and by the time I reach five you will all be wide awake, but you cannot leave this stage because your left foot is glued and stuck to the floor. Ready, One—two—three —four—and **five**. Everyone wide, wide awake.

"Allow me at this time to thank each of you for your splendid co-operation and powers of concentration, and now if you will try and return to your seats, please."

The subjects start to leave the stage, and are stopped suddenly in complete bewilderment at finding their left foot stuck to the floor. Confusion reigns supreme as they pull and tug trying to free their foot. You pass to each and snap your fingers by their ear; their left foot comes free, but the right is now stuck fast to the stage. More finger snapping, and first one foot and then the other gets stuck. Finally you slap your hands loudly beside one subject as you say, "All right, it's all gone. You are free," and he gingerly picks up his feet and marches off the stage. Free another subject, and then another. They march off the stage back to their seats in the audience. The next you release, you walk over with as though to escort him from the stage, and just when you get to the side pillar you suddenly place his hand flat against the wall, and say snarply, "Your hand is stuck there, you cannot pull it free." Having just been released from the post-hypnotic influence of having his foot stuck, he is still in a very responsive mood to the effects of suggestion, and his hand will get quickly stuck to the post. Leave him there tugging, and release another subject or so. Then walk towards the front of the stage, and just as one of your subjects is in the aisle to return to his seat ask him to turn around and look at you, and as he does so hold out your right forefinger and say, "Your eyes are fixed to the tip of my finger. See, you sway about as it sways. Your eyes are closing. You are sinking, sinking, your knees are sagging. Knees sagging. Dropping right down to the floor." The subject still in a hypnotic mood will instantly respond, begin to sway and sag down to his knees on the floor. Instantly, clap your hands and say, "All right, it's all gone now. You are wide, wide awake. Go back to your seat." Then dash quickly about the stage, release the subject stuck to the side post and all the rest of the subjects except one. Thus the stage is all clear with the exception of this last subject still tugging valiantly at his stuck leg. Him you ignore, as if, in your haste, you had absentmindedly overlooked him, and you give your concluding remarks to your audience,

"And so my friends you have witnessed a number of demonstrations of some of the unusual aspects of Hypnotism and on behalf of the volunteers and myself let me thank you for your most courteous attention."

All during these remarks, various members of the audience will be calling up trying to remind you that you have overlooked one subject on the stage. Suddenly seem to catch on, turn and spot the subject, and, with a brief apology, dash to him, clap your hands and release him. Walk with him to the side of the stage, shake him by the hand, thank him for his assistance, and let him return to his seat. Take your bow, and then **exit.**

This whole last sequence should be performed with as much dash and verve as you can manage to get into it. Heap action onto action. Lift your audience up to a fever pitch, and then the last humorous bit of seemingly overlooking the last subject gives you a marvelous finishing tag.

Of such is the makings of the hypnotic show.

FURTHER EXPERIMENTS IN HYPNOTISM

The hypnotic show just described is the one I personally use. Now, it is not expected that the performer will have occasion to make use of it just as it stands, for, as in Magic, the patter and presentation of one Magician would be entirely unsuited to another. **But the details of handling presented, the method of routining the hypnotic show illustrated, and the variety of effects offered will serve to give the Magician a detailed idea of how to arrange his own hypnotic show.** For further material, here described, is an additional variety of hypnotic effects. Since you now know the method, and have just studied the pattern in the giving of suggestions to produce the various hypnotic situation, we shall not give the details, but merely outline the general theme of each experiment in this chapter. The exact wording of the suggestion you can supply as necessary from your own practice and experience.

Drawing a Subject Across the Stage

This is an experiment in waking suggestion and fits in well with your "Falling Backward and Forward Tests."

Stand the subject at one extreme side of the stage. You stand at the opposite side, facing the subject. Stretch your hands out, at arms length, towards the subject, and while making pulling passes toward yourself, suggest that he is coming forward, that he will not fall, but will take a step forward, and, step by step, be pulled clear across the stage to you.

The Linked Hands Test

Another experiment in waking suggestion th
fits in splendidly with the test of "Locking the Hand
Together."

Have your group of subjects join hands together.
Suggest that their hands are becoming locked one to
the other, and that they cannot release their grips try
as hard as they will. The resulting struggle of the entire group striving to release their hands is most spectacular.

Going to Sleep in the Audience

You can cause quite a stir by giving a subject a
post-hypnotic suggestion that he will go to sleep the
moment he returns to his seat in the audience. When
he goes back to his seat and goes to sleep pretend not
to notice, and let the spectator tell you about it. Then
dash down to his side, and wake him up.

Age Regression

Tell your hypnotized subject that he is going back
through the years, and that he is now but two years
old, and is attending his second year birthday party.
The subject will act and respond exactly at a two-year
age level. This test can be made a feature in your show.

Age Advancement

Tell your hypnotized subject that he is going
ahead through the years, and that he is ninety years of
age, that he is stiff, and aged. Here is another feature
for your show that can be performed with the same

~bove experiment, making a logical

~rsonality Change

your hypnotized subject that he is some
~ry different from his normal personality,
~ newsboy, sailor, blustering politician, etc.
~sulting characterizations would do justice to a
~t polished actor.

Impersonation of Famous Persons

Tell your hypnotized subject that he is some famous movie star with which everyone is familiar, such
as Bing Crosby, as an example. The subject will impersonate expertly. You can interview him in his guise
of the star, have him sing, etc. In every case his reactions will be an interpretation of how the personality
he is impersonating would respond.

Singing and Playing an Instrument

Tell your hypnotized subject to sing or play a
musical instrument and he will oblige most willingly.
Unless he possesses actual talent you can hardly expect a concert, but his earnestness is most interesting
to watch.

Changing Sex

Tell a male subject that he is a woman, and then
place him in some female situation such as trying frantically to escape from a mouse. Conversely, tell a hypnotized female subject that she is a man, and is deliv-
ering a congressional speech. Tests of this nature
make fine demonstration for the stage.

Floor Pacing, and Continued Sleeping

Two hypnotic bits that you can use as running gags through your show are to hypnotize two subjects, and have one pace back and forth over at the side of the stage during the entire show, and place the second subject in a chair, on the opposite side of the stage, and leave him sleeping there throughout the entire proceedings.

The Chalk Line Test

Tell your hypnotized subject that he can not step over a chalk line which you draw on the stage. The subject is able to walk freely up to the line, but the moment he tries to step over it he is instantly blocked. This makes an interesting post-hypnotic experiment.

The Rubber Nose Test

Tell your hypnotized group of subjects that when they wake up their noses will be made of rubber, and that they can pull and stretch them out as long as they wish, yet when they let go, they will snap back right into their face. The resulting pantomime can well be imagined.

The Funny Audience Test

Here is another excellent post-hypnotic experiment to use with your entire committee. Tell them that when they awaken they will see all of the people in the audience looking very funny, with green and red spots all over them, ears like elephants, and necks like ostriches . . . that they never saw anything so funny in their lives, and that they will laugh and howl at that funny audience! When they awaken, at first they won't believe their eyes, but then they start, and how they do bellow. It's an irresistible test for any audience.

The Wonderful Penny Test

Place a penny in the palm of each of your hypnotized subjects, and suggest that it is getting very heavy, so heavy that they cannot lift it out of their palm as it is too heavy. The subjects will all pick at it, but it resists their efforts to lift it. Then say that the penny weighs all normal again, but that it is getting hot, very hot, and that they had better get rid of it before it burns their hand. The way they flip those pennies away and shake their hands is a riot.

The Hot Seat

A similar test to the latter part of the above, is to suggest to your subjects that the seat of their chair is getting very hot, and that they'd better get out of it pronto. Up they go with a yell!

The Water in the Pocket

Give a subject a glass of water and tell him it is a glass of peanuts, and that he must save them . . . so pour them into his pocket. In pours the glass of water. It's a "kick" test, but needless to say you must be careful with whom you work it. Use some good-natured boy wearing a pair of worn trousers, to whom a glass of water, more or less, is of little consequence in his young life.

The Flour Test

Bring forward a basin of flour and place it between two subjects. Tell them it is a basin of water, and to wash their hands in it. The results are easily guessed, but here again be careful of the subjects you choose for such a test.

The Mother and the Baby

A classical hypnotic experiment is to take two subjects and tell one that he is the mother and the other that he is the baby . . . the mother is to take the baby on her lap, sing it a lullaby, and rock it to sleep.

Experiments of this type always amuse an audience, but they must be presented in a spirit of good-natured humor so as not to ridicule the subjects.

The Imaginary Airplane Trip

Here you are building up a group hallucination for the entire committee. Tell them that they are all going on an aeroplane trip and are most enthusiastic about it. Then describe the trip, step by step, viz., leaving the ground, looking over the edge of the plane, sighting objects on the ground below, and the final landing. The individual responses of the different subjects as they react to the various suggested situations, according to their own natures, makes for a very spectacular test.

The Hot and Cold Test

A very strong experiment to present, is to suggest to your hypnotized group that they are getting very hot, that they are sitting near a hot stove in the middle of a desert with the blazing sun burning down on them. Tell them they simply must get cool, to open their collars, to take off their coats, etc. Some subjects will pick up and react to the entire situation entirely on their own, but in the majority of cases, better responses can be obtained by also directly suggesting the various little reactions desired.

When the subjects have become obviously hot enough, say, "Now the heat is all going away and you are becoming very cold, you are shivering. Put your coats back on and bundle up." This instant shift from hot to cold is a very spectacular demonstration.

The Swarm of Bees

Tell your hypnotized group of subjects that bees are beginning to buzz about their heads, to beat them off, and get away from them. It's confusing but amusing!

A Word to the Wise

Of course, it depends a great deal upon the performer's personality and his style of working, but **always show good taste in the hypnotic tests you present.** Hypnotic experiments from the past have been more-or-less of the type to put the subjects in ridiculous situations and make fools of them. For the sake of completeness a few such experiments are suggested in this chapter, but the modern approach to the hypnotic experiment is to use tests that, while amusing, show principles of Hypnotism and the variety of effects it can produce without directly poking fun at the subject. Naturally, the type of audience you are working before and the entertainment expected of you are factors in your deciding just what experiments are suitable. As an experienced showman, you can easily decide such problems, but, generally speaking, **make it your rule to never use experiments that would later make the subjects regret that they came forward upon the stage.** Remember, these subjects are free-will volunteers who came directly from the audience to the stage to help you. That implies a trust and confidence in you, and you must always respect that confidence to the utmost.

SENSATIONAL STUNTS

The modern Magician, ever on the lookout for the spectacular, will wish to include in his hypnotic program some feats that incite awe and speculation. Here, in this chapter, are presented a number of such experiments, from which you can draw in the building of your hypnotic show.

The Hypnotic Blood Test

For this test, use a fleshy, pink-skinned type of subject. Hypnotize him, roll back his sleeves, leaving the right arm bare, and have him stand erect with hands resting at his sides. Then tell him to clench his right hand tightly into a fist. As he does so, make contact passes up both sides of his arm from the wrist to the shoulder (See Fig. 60), and suggest, "Your arm is

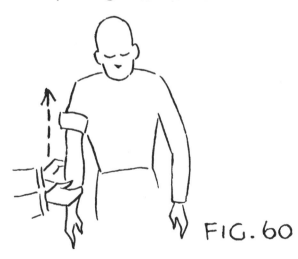

FIG. 60

becoming tense, the blood is leaving the arm. The blood is crawling up and up . . . up out of the arm." **Suddenly**

swing the arm upward in a circular motion to a hori-
zontal position, and suggest forcefully, "Arm and
shoulder muscles all stiff and rigid. **Stiff and rigid
The blood is all gone from your arm.**" (See Fig. 61)
The effect of these suggestions is to cramp the muscles of the arm and shoulder, driving the blood from
the arm.

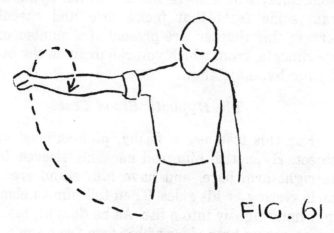

FIG. 61

You now tell your subject that while keeping the
arm perfectly rigid, to open out his fingers. The arm
is seen lifeless and white. Such is your reason for using
a subject of the fleshy type, as plump persons have a
transparency to their skins that emphasizes this effect
greatly.

The test completed, tell the subject to close his
hand again, that these muscles of his shoulders and
arm are becoming relaxed a bit, and that the blood will
flow back into the arm. As the muscles relax, the blood
will rush back coloring the arm brilliantly.

The Heart and Pulse Test

Hypnotize your subject, have one of the spectators
stand by his side and record the pulse beat as you sug-

gest, "Your heart will in a moment begin to beat slower and slower. Already it is commencing to slow down. It is beating slower and slower. I will count from one to three, and at the count of three your heart and pulse beat will be beating ever, ever slower. One—two—three. Your heart is beating very, very slow." Continue these suggestions until you have accomplished the degree of change you desire. The heart and pulse can then be speeded up by a reverse of the suggestions.

The degree of change is very marked, and the test very sensational especially to intelligent audiences. If possible have a physician keep track of the pulse beats and check on the changes in heart action.

The Pins Through the Flesh Test

Anaesthesia can be very readily induced while the subject is in the hypnotic trance. Have him raise his arm up horizontally, roll back the sleeve, make a few contact passes along the fleshy tissue at the side of his arm, and suggest, "All sensation is leaving your arm. There is no feeling in that arm at all . . . it is completely insensible. That arm feels all cold and dead. There is no feeling in your arm whatsoever." Repeat these suggestions several times, and lift up a fold of flesh and push a needle directly through (See Fig. 62).

Here are a few tips to aid you in successfully performing this feat. Never mention to the subject that you are going to pass a needle through his flesh, merely suggest that the arm feels all dead-like, and then perform the test without comment. Use a sharp needle and have a strong thread attached to it so that you can easily pull it out of the flesh. A thimble will assist in pushing it through. Pinch the flesh sharply between your thumb and forefinger just before you

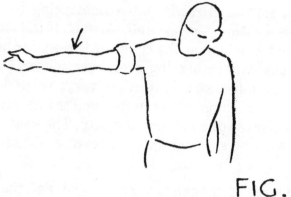

FIG. 62

pass the needle through. And always sterilize the needle by dipping it in antiseptic or burning in a match flame before using it in the test. The experiment, you will find, is a very easy one to perform, and is most helpful in convincing a skeptical audience of the genuineness of your phenomenon.

A long needle or hat pin can likewise be passed through the subject's cheek and out his mouth (See Fig. 63). This is not to be recommended, however, as is is always possible to injure the small nerves in the cheek.

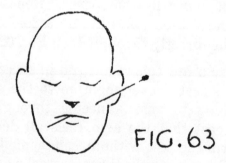

FIG. 63

Affecting the Senses of Taste and Smell

Here are a group of other very convincing tests

that testify strongly as to the reality of your phenomena.

Bring forward a bottle of concentrated ammonia, pass it out amongst the audience to prove its potent strength, then say to your hypnotized subject, "I am going to give you a bottle of very fragrant perfume. You will enjoy it very much. Smell it. It is positively delightful." Repeat these suggestions a few times to emphasize them. Then hand the bottle of ammonia to the subject and he will inhale it with every evidence of pleasure.

Next pour a glass full of vinegar. Let any who desire taste and test it. Then suggest, "I am going to give you a glass of very choice wine. You will enjoy it very, very much. What a pleasant aroma it has, what a delightful taste. Here sample it." The subject will swallow a mouthful of the vinegar with obvious enjoyment.

Then bring forth an onion and tell the subject that it is a luscious apple. Emphasize your suggestions of its goodness, how much he will enjoy eating it, etc., then give it to him. With complete enjoyment he will devour it.

Sensational tests of this type cannot be surpassed for proving beyond a shadow of a doubt that your tests are all on the level.

The Famous Cataleptic Rigid Test

The feat of rending the body rigidly supported between two chairs while you stand on the outstretched body was for years one of the main stock in trade effects of the old-time Hypnotists. You can accomplish the feat easily.

Deeply hypnotize your subject, have him stand upright with his feet tightly pressed together, then suggest, "Every muscle of your body is beginning to get stiff and rigid. As I pass my hand down your back to the top of your head to your heels your muscles will get stiffer and stiffer. Every muscle in your entire body is becoming stiff and rigid." Pass your hands down the back of the subject from the top of his head to his heels. You can judge how he is responding as you feel the muscles tensing beneath your fingers (See Fig. 64).

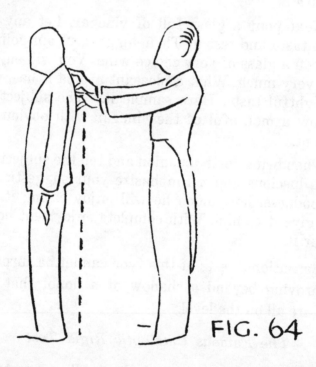

FIG. 64

Then go to the front of your subject, face him, place your hands on his shoulders and shout, "Rigid!" Follow right on through with a rapid fire of suggestion as, "Every muscle in your entire body is rigid. Nothing can make you bend. You are like a solid bar of iron. Nothing can make you bend. You are stiff and rigid as a bar of iron!"

Have a couple of spectators then help you lift the subject and place him across the back of two chairs which have been previously placed in position as shown in Fig. 65. Place the subject's ankles on one chair and the shoulder blades on the other. A pillow draped over the top of each chair will help in keeping them from cutting into the subject . . . **and remember you place the subject's shoulder blades on one chair, not the back of his head.** To expect those small muscles in the neck even though cataleptic, to support the entire weight of his body combined with your own is to ask too much.

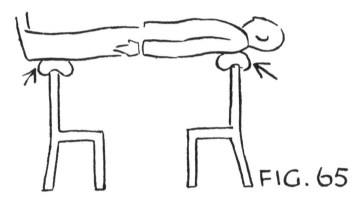

FIG. 65

Now with the help of a chair or a couple of spectators step directly and firmly up on top of the subject. Plant your weight firmly and evenly and do not shift about. One of your feet goes in the center of his chest and the other on the lower thigh (See 66).

You can stand on the subject thus as long as you wish, and when ready to come down, take the hand of a spectator and give a gentle leap to the floor. Have the subject removed from the chairs and stood upright, release him from the rigidity and awaken him. It is very important in this experiment to remove the rigidity gradually and completely, so be thorough about it as you suggest, "All right now, every muscle in your body is again becoming relaxed and at ease. Every bit of tense and stiffness is gone. And when you awake in just a moment you will feel refreshed and just good all over." Repeat these suggestions over and over a few times, and till you can see that every trace of tenseness is gone; then awaken the subject by the usual counting method.

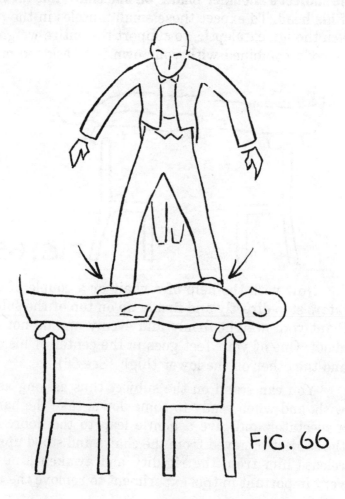

FIG. 66

The Rock Breaking Test

This is a variation of the Rigid Test and is often used in conjunction with it. The subject is hypnotized, rendered cataleptic, and placed outstretched between the two chairs as in the previous test. A felt pad is then draped over his chest and a large stone about three feet square and a foot in thickness placed directly on his chest (See Fig. 67). And then with a heavy blow or two from a sledge hammer the rock breaks and goes plunging to the stage with a series of loud thumps.

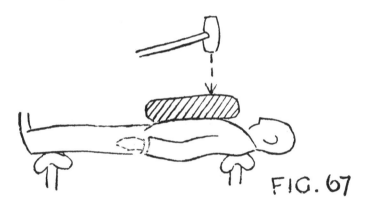

FIG. 67

The how of the test is almost automatic and with the exception of the induction of the catalepsy can hardly be called hypnotic, but it is so spectacular that it is very much worthwhile using. The rock is of sandstone and hence breaks quite readily. The felt pad over the chest of the subject takes some of the blow, and the inertia in the rock itself absorbs the large majority of it. Actually the subject experiences little more than a slight jar, and to the hypnotized subject such is not even noticed.

Hypnotizing the Entire Audience

Whenever you speak of hypnotizing the entire audience you are bound to create excitement. The feat is not too difficult to accomplish but you must be sure to have the undivided attention of the spectators, and even more important the spectators must understand that they are each individually trying the experiment and are to keep their attention on you and not keep looking about in curiosity as to how others nearby them may be effected. To conduct the experiment, stand facing your audience as you did your commitee, and address them,

"You have seen a number of experiments upon the stage now, and possibly you are all more or less curious as to just how it feels to be hypnotized. So, all together now we will try and enter the trance.

"For this test to be successful each of you must decide in your own mind that you sincerely wish to be hypnotized. And I will do my very best to help you pass down into the condition. One thing is very important, keep your attention fixed upon me at all times, concentrate upon the suggestions I give you, and **forget all about the rest of the audience.** Consider this an individual experiment between you and me, and do not take your gaze away from me at anytime to look towards other persons in the audience, for to do so will not only interfere with your own experience, but also with others in the audience.

"All ready everyone, sit back comfortably in your seats, place your feet flat on the floor, and rest one hand on each knee. Now direct your gaze towards me, directly toward my eyes."

Lift up your hands and make large sweeping

passes towards the audience, and swing slowly from one side to the other so that your eyes take in the entire audience in a sweep from left to right. Having completed the first sweeping arc with your eyes, sweep them back slowly from right to left this time, and continue thus back and forth until the eyes of everyone are closed (See Fig. 68).

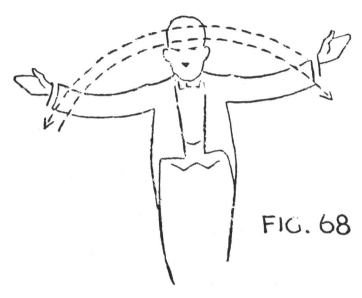

FIG. 68

Then proceed to hypnotize, working exactly as you did with the entire committee on the stage; eliminating the group breathing however, and proceed on as rapidly as you can to getting the eyes closed. In working with the entire audience get everyone's eyes closed as fast as you are able and then suggest,

"Now that your eyes are closed, blackness begins to surge about you, and you feel a drawing towards the back of your head. Your heads are tipping back. Your chins are coming up, and your head is tipping back, back against the rear of your seat. You are getting so sleepy. Heads all tipping back, settle down more in your seats and rest your heads against the back of your seat."

You can tell right here how well your audience as a whole is responding. For if they are following your suggestions their heads will slowly begin to tilt back, and when you say "settle down more in your seats" there will be a general rustling as they snuggle down. If enough are responding, follow through with the "sleep formula" sending them down, deeper and deeper to sleep. If not sufficient number are co-operating to make the test worthwhile, quickly arouse them and say, "There, that will serve to give you a brief idea of a bit of the relaxation that Hypnotism can bring." Then forget all about the test and proceed right on to your other experiments.

Let us assume, however, that the test is proving successful and that many in the audience have co-operated fully, proceed then until they are well entranced, and then bring it to a conclusion with, "All right you are all resting calmly now, sleeping peacefully and quiet. These few moments of concentrated rest are doing you a great deal of good. Every muscle, or organ in your entire body is being refreshed, and when you awaken in just a moment you will feel better than you have at anytime this entire week. And here is something important. Tonight, after you leave this hall and go to bed, you will go to sleep instantly. The moment your head touches the pillow you will go instantly to sleep. And when you awake in the morning you will say that it was the best sleep you have ever had. Real deep, refreshing sleep."

This gives the audience in whatever hypnotic condition they happen to be whether deep trance or merely relaxed, something to look forward to. Then conclude the test by awaking everyone as a group using the familiar method of slowly counting from one to five.

You will find this experiment of hypnotizing the entire audience a very effective test to use on the right occasion, and that many, many persons will respond to it. Do not, however, try any especial tests on the hypnotized spectators . . . let your induction of the sleep and the hypnotic mood suffice.

Super-Normal Stage Experiments in Hypnotism

We come now to a group of experiments the results of which are problematical. Many operators say they work splendidly, so experiment with them. However, as is always the case in working with the more subtle side of hypnosis, never expect success at every attempt.

Take five playing cards and lay them face downward on the table. Bring forward your hypnotized subject, place the palm of his hand on the back of the card, and command him to name it. He will do so, and you can check on the correctness by lifting up the card so all can see. Repeat the test several times.

Take a hat and collect a number of articles from about ten different spectators. Have the spectators drop the articles in the hat themselves and do not touch them yourself. Then give the hat to the subject and command him to pick up each article in turn and take it back to its owner. Some subjects will start right out, others you will have to aid slightly by taking their hand and going along with them. But once they get started, the subject will experience no trouble in returning all of the objects correctly.

Try now an experiment in telepathic hypnotism. Hypnotize your subject very deeply, and suggest that his mind is free of all thoughts, and then that he is to visualize the room he is performing in with his eyes closed. Tell him he can see you easily, can see the spectators, and is acutely aware of everything going on about him. Then suggest that you are going to send impulses to him of various things he is to perform by telepathy. Explain that his instructions will come in the form of mental pictures in his mind, and that he is to do exactly as the pictures direct.

Then go into the audience and have different spectators whisper different tests that they would like the subject to perform, such as go to a blackboard and make a mark, remove his right shoe, take off his coat, etc. Having decided on a test, shout up to the subject on the stage, "Ready, I am concentrating. Receive my thought and do as the picture that is forming in your mind directs." In many cases the subject will respond correctly.

As always in tests of this nature, the success of the experiment depends upon the subject's innate E.S.P. ability, so results are bound to vary. Your own mental attitude is important also; you must feel completely confident in your own mind that the subject will respond, and that if he does not then you will merely try again. Your attitude in such tests must be that of the scientific investigator rather than the magical entertainer.

The two tests next to be described are in the nature of publicity stunts that the Hypnotist will find very effective in exploiting his entertainment. Both are very easily handled and are conducive to creating much talk.

Hypnotizing via Radio

In private, hypnotize your subject, and knowing that he is readily responsive to your influence you are ready for the test.

In the window of some store have a large comfortable chair, and beside it a radio turned to the local station. Under the observation of a committee the subject is led to the chair and he seats himself.

You meanwhile are at the radio station, and when the time comes for your broadcast, the announcer first explains where the subject is now located in the window of such and such a store, and that over the air waves you will attempt to hypnotize the subject. You then come on the air and hypnotize the subject directly via radio.

Naturally since you have previously hypnotized the subject it is a very simple matter to entrance him as your voice comes in over the radio, but don't make it seem too simple. Rather keep your "sleep formula" going as long as seems advisable. **However, be certain that you explain in your opening instructions that you will be able to influence only the one subject through this unusual medium, otherwise the station is liable to be getting phone calls in from all over the place frantically asking you to come and awake sleeping persons.** This is really a serious point, so remember it in staging your routine.

Since the hypnosis you induce on the subject in the window is entirely genuine, doctors, psychologists, and any others who wish can test his reaction as they desire. The progressive Magician can readily see the great publicity value of this test. It presents opportunities for unlimited bally.

The Window Sleep

This venerable experiment has made the reputation of many a performer. Briefly the effect is that at such and such a time you are announced to appear in the window of some store to conduct a demonstration in Hypnotism. Comes the time for the demonstration a large crowd usually awaits your appearance and you enter the window with the subject. **Use a girl for this test.** The subject is then hypnotized, placed in a bed on display in the window and is left any number of hours that is desired. At the agreed upon period you return and awaken the subject who is none the worse for her long sleep.

The method is as straightforward as is the description of the effect. The subject is genuinely hypnotized and is put to bed. Give suggestion that she will continue sleeping on down deeper and deeper with the passing of each moment, and will not awaken until you come to awaken her. Emphasize this fact, that no person or things can awaken her under any conditions until you wake her up personally, and suggest that every noise she hears of any type will only serve to keep sending her down deep, deep to sleep. Thus the test is accomplished. When the time comes to awaken the subject, enter the window and remove the trance just as in any other hypnotic experiment.

Some little points that will assist you in smoothly staging the experiment are to be sure that everything in the window is arranged for the comfort of the subject. If the window is cold, have a heater. If the window is hot, have a fan. Always cover the subject's body up lightly so that only her head shows. Do not prolong the test over six hours, starting say at noon and concluding the experiment at six in the evening. Occasionally you can make it last a few hours longer, taking the subject in an ambulance from the window through the streets to the theatre where it is announced that you will awaken her on the stage. Actually the length of time the subject sleeps makes little difference hypnotically speaking, simply return to the window every hour or so and give further suggestions that the subject is comfortable and is sleeping soundly. Suggest also that the subject may turn over in bed if she wishes. **Do everything in your power to promote the subject's comfort in every way.**

Window Sleeps have been conducted for as long as a seven-day period without harm to the subject, but for all practical purposes a six-hours' sleep will provide you with ample publicity. You will be amazed at the talk and comments a person innocently sleeping in a store window will evoke.

HYPNOTIC MISDIRECTION

Misdirection in Magic is to deceive the eye; misdirection in Hypnotism is to deceive the mind, and through its skillful application hypnosis can frequently be induced without the subject's awareness—a procedure often of great value to the magical entertainer.

Perhaps the most classical example of hypnotic misdirection is the physician who gives his patient "sugar pills" under the guise that they are sleeping tablets. The patient takes the "pills" and experiences exactly the same effects as that produced by an actual opiate.

Another illustration of such disguised hypnotic technique is cited by George Estabrooks, he writes, "To hypnotize the subject without his realizing what is happening, we ask his co-operation in a harmless little psychological experiment using some piece of psychological apparatus as a front behind which to work. Perhaps the simplest is the device for measuring blood pressure. We explain to the subject that we wish to test his ability to relax, and we can measure this by his blood pressure. That sounds very reasonable so we fix the rubber band on his arm, tell him to close his eyes and relax all his muscles.

"We further explain that, of course, the deepest form of relaxation is sleep, and that if the subject can fall asleep it will show that he has perfect control over his nervous system. Then we proceed to 'talk sleep' much the same as in Hypnotism, being careful to avoid any references to trances, seances, or Hypnotism, and omitting all tests except one. After five minutes, during which period we have checked several times on the blood pressure to keep up the delusion, we tell the subject that we would like to see if he can talk in his sleep, since this represents the very deepest form of relaxation. If he does, he is in deep hypnosis. The experiment can be even further simplified by merely using a watch to take the subject's pulse with the explanation that it is to check on his relaxation."

An important principle in applying these hypnotic misdirection techniques for the Magician is to attach significance to some mystical object as having a degree of power which the subject will respond to.

For The Private Entertainment — The Crystal Ball Method

Next time you have a parlor program, introduce the psychically interested subject to your crystal ball, tell him of its marvelous properties as you weave a yarn of Oriental enchantment about its subtle influence over some persons, explaining that it will actually entrance people of a psychical disposition. Aim your patter so as not to arouse a desire to resist the influence, but rather make him feel privileged at being able to work with your crystal ball and increase his desire to prove that he does indeed possess psychic powers through passing this test of having the crystal entrance him.

Next, explain to the subject exactly how he is to use the crystal, viz, he is to place it on a table in front of him, sit back comfortably in a chair and center his eyes on it (See Fig. 69). Then he is to gaze directly at the ball, on past the reflections into its very depths. Explain that if he is doing the experiment correctly the ball will gradually become darker and a sort of milky mist will form in front of his eyes, between the

FIG 69

crystal and himself. This mist will grow and grow until it completely engulfs him. He is then to let his mind float out in this mist until blackness envelopes all. And with the blackness will come a complete state of phychic entrancement.

In this experiment don't mention either sleep or hypnotism; keep your patter entirely centered on the subject's desire to test his own psychic powers.

When all is understood and your subject is in an eager mood to test his powers of psychic responsiveness by using your remarkable crystal ball, have him enter a semi-darkened room, alone, and close the door. Twenty minutes later you enter softly, and in many cases you will find the subject seated in the chair with his eyes either closed or staring blankly into space—completely entranced. Speak to him quietly, and if he answers you without arousing, you can rapidly bring him under your hypnotic control.

For the Stage Show — The Magic Wand Method

Here is a natural for the Magician. Sometime when you have an eager, willing and nervous lad upon the stage to assist you with some trick, introduce him to your magic wand. Tell him it possesses remarkable magic powers and that it can make him do all kinds of wonderful and unusual things. Then offer to show him how it works.

Having aroused his interest, ask him to focus his eyes on the shiny metal tip of one end of the wand, explaining that he is to keep his eyes riveted on that tip at all times and to follow it wherever you move it in order to absorb some of the magic powers through his optic nerve. Hold the wand in your right hand about eight inches from his face directly on the level of his eyes (See Fig. 70).

FIG. 70

Now grip the back of his head firmly with your left hand, and move the wand upward in a slow arc (See Fig. 71). Since you are holding the subject's head rigidly so that it cannot move, only his eyes will turn upward, and when they reach a point where the pupil is almost hidden behind the upper lid, they will suddenly blink shut. At this point bring the wand down level with his eyes again, and repeat this up and down motion with the wand ten or twelve times. The last time the eyes blink, tell him to keep his eyes shut tight.

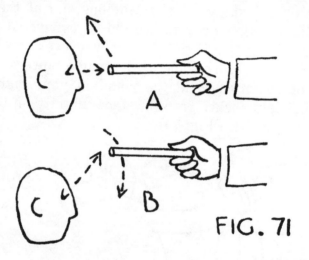

FIG. 71

Now place your wand so it touches the center of his head, and tell him to roll his eyes upward under the closed lids as though he were looking back into his skull towards the very point that the wand is touching. Tell him to keep looking upward as you press the wand firmly against the top of his head, and suggest that his eyelids are getting stuck so tightly together by the magic power of the wand that he cannot open them, try as hard as he will. Keep a string of suggestions constantly going directly into his ear, **always associating his responses as being due to properties in**

the magic wand itself rather than anything hypnotic.

As you perform this eyelid fastening technique, move your left hand down from the back of the subject's head and press inward at the very nape of his neck at the top of the spinal column. Press very firmly (See Fig. 72). This produces a deadening sensation through his entire body, and once his eyes have proved themselves fastened against his efforts to open them, it takes but very little suggestion,—"Now the magic wand is making you very sleepy. Its power is seeping into your brain and is making you go sound asleep right on your very feet. Etc.—to send the subject rapidly into a deep hypnotic trance.

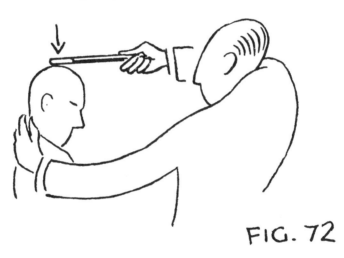

FIG. 72

Dr. Q's Hypnotic Act

My very good friend, Bill Larsen, very kindly gave me permission to include this act. On first reading the Magician may wonder what a fraudulent method of hypnotizing is doing in an encyclopedia of genuine methods. Once you have tried working the routine, however, you will understand, because the principle employed in the Dr. Q. Act of "direct cueing" is an excellent example of hypnotic misdirection. So subtle is the transfer from voluntary action to involuntary that it would take a highly skilled psychologist to spot the shift.

As the principle is used in the present instance; we shall consider Dr. Q.'s Hypnotic Act as an approach to Stage Hypnotism where the subjects are led to believe they are merely assisting you entertain the audience, never realizing that they are opening their minds to actually entering a hypnotic condition. Of such is the misdirection of hypnotic misdirection.

You commence the act by giving the audience a brief speech on Hypnotism.

"And now, friends, let us turn our thoughts for a few moments to the wonder science of the human mind —Hypnotism. The study of Hypnotism has claimed human thought for centuries, but it has only been in comparatively recent years that a real appreciation of its marvels have come to be recognized. For, as you have undoubtedly read in the many current articles now appearing, Hypnotism is currently being practiced in our foremost hospitals and colleges with almost miraculous results both curatively and psychologically.

"Tonight, in just a moment, I am going to invite a few volunteers up on this stage to participate in some demonstrations in this remarkable phenomenon called Hypnotism.

"First, however, I should like to remove the old superstition that to be hypnotized a person must have a weak mind. Such has now been proved by science to be a complete fallacy. Indeed, some of the very best hypnotic subjects have been persons of very high intelligence, and vivid, creative imaginations. So, tonight, when you volunteer for these demonstrations, you may rest assured that you are placing yourself amongst the very best of intellectual company.

"You see, Hypnotism is not something dark and mysterious. To explain it simply, and to phrase it in psychological terms, it is purely a state of mind produced through the influence of suggestion—the power of ideas.

"Now, when you volunteer to come up on this stage to participate in these demonstrations, I want every person to realize that I shall treat them with the utmost courtesy and respect. And, by the same token, I merely ask that you give me your earnest co-operation and attention.

"And now, without further ado, I wish to invite a few of you gentlemen up on this stage to experiment with Hypnotism. Will four or five, or possibly even more, gentlemen kindly step forward? Thank you, sirs."

You will find that this introduction convinces your audience almost instantly that you know your subject, and makes them realize that there is indeed something to Hypnotism. Also, these opening remarks place the volunteers completely at ease in coming up on the stage, removes them from any later criticism of being weak-minded, and places them in a frame of mind to work along with you. Thus your introduction has not only secured for you co-operative volunteers, but likewise sold your audience on the reality of what you are about to attempt.

The Dr. Q. Hypnotic Method

Having secured four or five volunteers on the stage, have them stand in a row about two feet apart. Go to the one on the left end of the line (as you face them), and turning your back deliberately on the audience, place your left hand on the back of his neck, at the base of the brain, and **squeeze gently**, but at the same time **firmly**.

In assuming this position you will be facing the subject squarely, so look him directly and earnestly in the eyes while your free right hand makes gentle pass-like gestures in the air, and you **whisper** (simply speak in a low, soft voice . . . this will carry clearly to the subject will not reach the ears of the spectators in the audience) **to him:** "We are going to have some good laughs on the audience and fool them . . . so when I tell you to do some funny things, do exactly as I secretly tell you. O.K.? Swell!" (Then deliberately wink at the spectator in a friendly fashion.)

The psychological affect of such a proceeding is to render the man a willing dupe to your ends. Your stance, with the pressure upon his neck puts you in a position of dominance. This coupled with your position as "master of the stage" will render him amenable to do exactly what you tell him.

Then, too, your words to him are in the nature of a "whispered confidence" of producing laughs on the rest of the spectators in the audience. The volunteer thus begins to feel important that he is in on a secret, and is to become "part of the show."

Your bold "O.K.? Swell!" . . . implies his automatic acceptance of willingness to follow your instructions, and your parting **wink** cinches the spirit of "good fellowship" between you. Handled thus, any spectator who happens to come up on the stage quickly becomes "a perfect hypnotic subject" for your demonstrations. Dr. Q is certainly to be commended for developing this perfectly brilliant psychological method of "handling" the subjects.

Proceed next to the second spectator in the row, and repeat exactly your instructions. Take the same stance with him, and say the same words—just as you did with the first subject. Possibly this second spectator may have heard a bit of what you whispered to the first person. If so, he will simply "catch on" that much quicker.

Then go to the third spectator and proceed likewise with him. Just before you leave, however, whisper, "After I shake your hand and let go—make your palm stick to mine."

Step a bit to his side, and, as though it were a friendly parting gesture, take his right hand in yours and shake it. Move the hands around a bit, and then **open your fingers, at the same time pressing your palm tightly against his. Push your palm up so it forces his arm back.** This tends to "set" your whispered instructions in his mind, so when you now pull your hand down, as though to take it away, he will follow right along with you exactly as if his palm were really glued to your own.

This is very funny, and in a second's time the fun will commence, and the volunteer will begin to get a "big kick" out of all the laughs he's creating and will really stick to your hand in earnest, just as though it were actually hypnotically stuck. If you wish, you can even try shaking your hand free from his, but he'll follow right along—stuck tight! The audience will

howl! Then suddenly give him a tap on the neck (as though snapping him out of the hypnotic influence), and with a loud "All right," jerk your hand free.

This demonstration, funny as it is in itself, is performed at this time, for a very important purpose. It shows the other volunteers the kind of actions that are going to be expected of them . . . and thus gets them all **expectant** awaiting to follow your whispered commands.

Then quickly proceed to your next volunteers and give them the same whispered instructions to do whatever you tell them . . . you are now ready to go into the Hypnotic Routine.

First, however, let us consider for a moment just what has been the audience's reaction to all of this. **To them it looks like you are hypnotizing the subjects,** and since that is what they are expecting you to be doing it all passes naturally. The audience sees your stern position as you gaze into the eyes of the man, the mysterious passes your right hand is making in the air, and even the mumble of whispers seems to them the expected "hypnotic formula" used in hypnotizing.

Since you are whispering so softly that only the subject you are directly in front of can clearly hear your words, the audience has no chance whatsoever of knowing what you are saying . . . and since they have no idea as to just what is going to happen, they have no cause for the least bit of suspicion. Their attitude is one of eager interest, waiting for something amusing to happen.

The whole "hypnotizing" proceedings with the first two subjects takes place so rapidly that it is completed before anyone has had much chance to give it critical thought. And then, the funny demonstration with the "stuck hand" is such a big laugh that it covers up the little remainder of the time it takes to get to the rest of the subjects in the line.

After that first test, the spectators will be more than ever on their toes, eager and expectant, to see more of your "Hypnotism."

This building of audience acceptance is another ingenious aspect of the Doctor's Hypnotic Method . . . for not only does it psychologically handle the subjects on the stage, but it also psychologically handles the audience.

Dr. Q's Own Hypnotic Routine

Having instructed each of the volunteers secretly, as has been described, Dr. Q next would dash back to the first spectator in the line and whisper, "When I clap my hands fall down." He would give these quick instructions in a flash without even so much as stopping in front of the party, and then pass right on to the second spectator in the line.

Pausing before this spectator he would raise his hands and clap them, and the **first spectator would fall down.** While clapping his hands thus, and during the laugh on this unexpected occurrence, he would whisper to the second spectator, "When I pick him up, you fall down."

The Doctor would then rush over to the first spectator and pick him up from the floor, and the **second spectator falls down.** As he picks up the first spectator he whispered, "When I pick up this other fellow you fall down again." Then picking up the second spectator, **the first would fall down again.**

He would then shout loudly, "All right, all right

... it's all gone!" and go over and help the first subject back on his feet.

It is impossible to describe how funny this demonstration appears to the audience. You will just have to try it to appreciate its value. You'll find that your audience will positively howl . . . and the more they howl, the better your subjects will respond to your whispered instructions.

Dr. Q, during this laughter on his "Falling Test," would go to the third subject (the one he had previously used in the "Hand Sticking") and shake his hand while he whispered, ·"Make our hands stick again." And the subject's hand would become again stuck to his. Dr. Q would then bend over, and placing the subject's right hand flat on the floor would go through the motions of nailing it to the stage while he whispered, "Make it stick there."

The subject would then vainly try to pull his hand free, until the Doctor hit him gently on the back of the neck as he said loudly, "All right, it's all gone now!"

While the subject was trying to pull his hand free of the stage, Dr. Q would go to the fourth subject in the line, and while standing directly in front of this spectator would request him to open his mouth wide. He would then whisper for him to keep it open as though it were impossible to get it closed. Stepping aside, **the audience would see the subject with his mouth stuck wide open.** Dr. Q would even tell the subject to try hard to close it with his hands.

Few things could be funnier, and the audience howled louder than ever with laughter. During this laughter, Dr. Q would release the subject pulling on his hand stuck to the stage, and rapidly move on to the last subject in the row. Standing in front of this man he would raise the subject's right hand and place its thumb against the man's nose, while he quickly whispered, "Hold it stuck there." **The subject would then appear to try in vain to get his thumb away from the end of his nose.**

Quickly Dr. Q would leave this last subject with his thumb stuck to his nose, dash over to the first subject in the row, and lead him over to the side of the stage or wall. **Placing his hand against the wall,** he'd whisper, "Keep it stuck."

Dashing back to each of the remaining subjects on the stage, he'd command each in turn to **open their mouths wide,** and then a whispered cue to "Keep it stuck."

By this time, there is so much action heaped each upon the other, and the audience is laughing so loudly that you will find in working the act that you can almost give your instructions out loud. In fact, your subjects will so have caught on to what is expected of them, and be having such a swell time in making the audience laugh that they'll do anything you suggest at the slightest provocation. Indeed, you can abolish the whispered instructions almost entirely and proceed right into the role of a Hypnotist giving suggestions as: "Open your mouth wide. It is stuck, you cannot close it!" As you look steadily at the subject while giving such suggestions, give him a **wink.**

Dr. Q would thus go from subject to subject until he had **a row on the stage standing with their mouths stuck wide open.** Then going quickly to each one, he'd apparently snap them out of it by a gentle tap and a loud, "All right, it's all gone!" At the same time he'd whisper to each, "When I clap my hands fall down."

Dr. Q then would thank the subjects for volunteering to help in the demonstrations, and ask them to return to their seats. As they left the stage he'd watch them carefully, and when some were in the aisles and others on the stairs, he'd clap his hands together loudly ... **and the subjects would fall down in a heap wherever they happened to be!** Thus providing a perfect climax for a perfect act.

The foregoing is the exact hypnotic routine as performed by the celebrant Dr. Q. of course, the reader can work out his own routine in any number of countless variations, for in applying this method numerous tests will suggest themselves to you. However, don't make the mistake of performing too many demonstrations. Just do a few and let it go at that. Frankly, it is to be doubted that Dr. Q's own routine can be very much improved upon. Performed with showmanship, it will positively provide a few minutes of utter amazement and humor that an audience will never forget.

Before proceeding on to Dr. Q's Challenge Hypnotic Method, attention should be called to the very subtle manner in which the Dr. Q methods present the whispered instructions—note how all instructions are given under cover of some larger action, and how all instructions tend to be "one-ahead" of their occurrence ... so, that while the audience is laughing at one stunt a new one is being set. Thus, when it later transpires it appears to occur spontaneously.

Challenge Hypnotism

Occasionally, although very rarely, you may run up against a person who is refractory about entering into the situation with you and following your instructions. Dr. Q would always get around any such difficulty by applying the following secret method of putting the subject to sleep **against his will.** This is the famous "Bulldog Method" which has long been one of the most cherished secrets of stage Hypnotists.

Standing directly in front of the subject, push his head well back, with your left hand on the front of his forehead. Then place the thumb and first finger of your right hand directly on his exposed throat, just above the Adam's apple. You can quickly find the exact spot by the feel of the blood pounding through the veins in his throat beneath your fingers. Push firmly in upon these veins, at the same time requesting the man to breathe deeply. (Even if he doesn't wish to comply, he'll be largely compelled to do so in order to get air in such a position.) Maintain this pressure upon the veins in his throat for a moment, and at the same time push his head farther backward . . . and carefully watch your subject. (See Fig. 73).

You will find that he will suddenly **go limp.** Catch this moment and shout loudly, **"Sleep,"** **and let him drop to the floor in a heap.**

Step aside to give the audience a chance to see the "hypnotized" man on the floor. Then quickly bend over the subject and hit him gently on the back of the neck while saying in a loud voice, "All right now, wake up now . . . wide awake!"

After that demonstration you will find that subject will be most docile and willing to follow whatever whispered instructions you care to give. It also serves to impress the other subjects on the stage to the end that they'd better co-operate along with you—**or else.**

This Challenge Method works through the device of cutting the blood flow to the brain, and thus saturating the brain with carbon dioxide—producing un-

FIG. 73

consciousness. Avoid using the test on persons with heart trouble of any kind, and always **handle it with caution.** As soon as the subject goes limp, release your pressure upon the veins in his neck, and let him drop to the floor. Since the effect of the unconsciousness only lasts a short time, for effect, bend over the subject and seemingly snap him out of the "hypnotic trance" before he comes-to of his own accord.

Unexpected Hypnosis

Hypnotic misdirection is applied in this type of experiment to bring the subject suddenly into the trance while his attention is actually focused on performing another type of suggestive phenomena.

With the Falling Experiment: In performing the test of "Drawing the Subject Over Backward," if he responds readily, as he falls back into your arms, suddenly suggest forcefully and loudly, "Keep your eyes closed, closed tight shut, and **sleep! Go sound, sound to sleep!**" In many cases, the subject, stimulated by wonder and bewilderment at his response to the "Falling Test," will instantly pass into profound hypnosis.

With the Hand Clasping Experiment: Having locked your subject's hands tightly together, and while he is straining to take them apart, rather than releasing those hands with a snap of your fingers, ask him to again look directly into your eyes, and you suggest, "Your hands are stuck and they will not come apart. Now your eyes too are getting heavy, the lids are closing and they too will get stuck tightly together. So tightly that you cannot open them any more than you can take those stuck hands apart. Close your eyes. Close them tight. The lids are stuck, **stuck!** You cannot open them try as hard as you will. **Try, try hard!**" (The subject tries in vain to open his stuck eyelids.) Now forget all about your eyes, forget all about your hands. Those stuck hands are relaxing and coming apart. Your arms and hands are relaxing and are falling to your sides, and by the time they reach your sides you will be sound to sleep. **Sleep!**" Follow with some "sleep formula." This method is extremely effective for rapidly producing hypnosis directly from a test in the waking state.

The Toothache Method: While passing in front of one of your subjects as he sits in a chair among the committee, suddenly look into his eyes and tap him under his jaw with the fingers of your right hand and state very emphatically that he has a toothache. Don't hold your fingers still, but keep on tapping the jaw firmly, without, however, removing the fingers. Continue to tell him that he has a toothache and that it hurts him badly, all the time looking him directly in the eyes. Soon he will jump up with a howl. Now quickly catch his attention, telling him that his toothache is gone, but to close his eyes and go to sleep. Following then with a few suggestions of "Sleepy, sleepy, you are going to sleep" are all that are necessary to place him in a deep hypnotic sleep.

These methods of unexpectedly inducing hypnosis while not practical to use universally for first hypnotic results, when applied at the right time and with the right subjects are among the fastest methods of hypnotizing yet discovered.

THE INNER SECRETS OF
STAGE HYPNOTISM

The principles considered in this chapter are so basic to the entire field of Hypnotism that we are bound to cover some ground already discussed, but the application of these secrets is the real key to your success as a Stage Hypnotist.

Most contemporary critics on things hypnotic for the stage seem to regard such Hypnotism as being 90 per cent trickery and 10 per cent suggestion. Actually, it would seem to be nearer the truth if those figures were reversed. Obviously such beliefs are a hangover from the **old** Stage Hypnotism where the whole act was purely a rehearsed stage project employing a company of trained confederates. However, the modern approach to Stage Hypnotism is different, and, as was commented on in the Dr. Q Act, even when the subjects are first given direct cues, there soon arises a point where it is almost impossible to tell which responses are deliberate on the part of the subject and which are involuntary. **As a Stage Hypnotist, entertainment is your chief aim, and towards that end all of your efforts should be directed.**

Expectancy

Here lies one of the great secrets of Stage Hypnotism—the expectancy of your subjects on the stage to be hypnotized by you. Psychologically speaking such is, of course, the real producer of all of the phenomena, for if the subjects keenly **expect** to be hypnotized they are two-thirds of the way into the trance before you even start. **Thus every stimuli you present must be aimed to arouse to greater and greater heights that expectancy.** The process starts with your advertising before the subjects even come to the show. It continues to build on through your opening lecture as they come forward to the stage. It develops further as each test proceeds, and finally climaxes in the actual hypnotizing of the subject. Since all of these factors are entirely under the control of the operator, the performing of Stage Hypnotism, through the cultivation of the proper expectancy, can become almost as controlled performance as that of Magic.

The Stage Situation

This is one of the major advantages the stage operator enjoys over any other type of Hypnotist, for there is a certain atmosphere about the stage that is extremely conducive to the successful demonstrating of Hypnotism. The lights, the music, the curtains, the tenseness of being on the stage, and above all the expectancy centered on each subject by the audience— expectancy that he will be hypnotized, are factors working so powerfully in the performer's favor that hypnotism under such conditions is actually more readily accomplished than under any other. **It is because of this "stage situation" that Hypnotism can be induced on the stage with greater speed than in any other situation.**

Importance of Importance

Few things are more essential to the Stage Hypnotist than to act on this phrase, "The Importance of Importance." For the more important you make your work appear the greater will be your success. So observe three rules, i.e., make the state of Hypnotism, itself, important; make the audience feel that your performance of Hypnotism is important; and make your subjects feel that being hypnotized is important. How much more readily you can accomplish those rules with a dignified semi-scientific presentation instead of the antiquated approach of the hypnotic show as a series of ridiculous stunts.

Social Approval

If you have sold your audience completely on Hypnotism as a superior mental state of great value, you can realize the superior light in which such will place your subjects. For, far from being regarded as weak-willed stooges, they become courageous experimenters. Aim all of your work towards building the social approval of both Hypnotism and your subjects entering hypnosis. In direct ratio to the amount of social approval which you develop, will be your success as a Hypnotist.

No Challenge

Your entire presentation must always be to cultivate a response of "No Challenge" from both the spectators and the subjects. The nature of Hypnotism and the perpetuated beliefs that the performer masters and dominates the weaker wills of his subjects are things you must overcome. To have to push constantly uphill against such prejudice is to ruin both the effectiveness of your show and your hypnotic results. Therefore, you must almost "bend over backwards" to conduct yourself in such a way as to convey "No Challenge." Your attitude is that of the teacher instructing students in the learning of a skill.

Subject Responsibility

Lay the entire proceedings of the show directly in the laps of the subjects themselves, and make them responsible for the show's success. Frankly state the truth that the ability to be hypnotized lies entirely with the subject, and that your part is purely to assist them, as expertly as you are able, in entering the state ... then let the subjects assume all of the responsibility for the results. The human factor in hypnotizing is bound to bring you face to face with failure occasionally, but you can save yourself from embarrassment in such moments if you are seemingly impersonal about the results obtained. If you succeed in a test be very matter of fact about it, and always congratulate the subject letting him take the credit. If a test fails, be equally unconcerned and either repeat the experiment or proceed calmly on to another test. Just keep in mind that if a failure does not bother you that the audience will not be bothered by it either.

On Taking Bows

Applause in the hypnotic show should always be spontaneous. If they give you an ovation, acknowledge it of course, but never deliberately pull for applause by a bow after each test. Rather go directly from one experiment on into the next keeping your show moving rapidly. And don't feel too disappointed if you don't get too much applause. Hypnotism is very much like Magic in this regard, the subject matter tends to absorb the audience's attention to a degree that their interest abstracts them. The after-the-show talk is what you really want.

Routine

Exactly as in Magic the manner in which you routine your show forms a large factor in its success. So develop a hypnotic routine of effects that seem to produce the best results and proves the most entertaining to the audience, then learn that routine thoroughly and stick to it. A few variations every so often are of course permitted, but for the most part get your patter and presentation so thoroughly routined that you follow it automatically. You have enough distractions in holding the audience's interest, the committee's attention, and hypnotizing all at the same time without having to worry about an imperfectly mastered routine as well.

Group Size, Age, and Sex

Don't have less than a dozen chairs on the stage, or more than twenty-five. **About twenty is ideal.** And in inviting the committee to the stage specify, "No children please, persons of high school age or older." This is not because children do not make hypnotic subjects as they are excellent once you capture their imaginations, but in a mixed group a child makes the older members feel a little foolish in responding to suggestions when a child does likewise. **So keep the children off the stage.** The majority of your committee will be composed of high school and college age students, and they make a splendid group with which to work. **Ask both sexes to come forward.** The girls will be a little hesitant at first, but a little coaxing soon gets a number up. **A mixed committee composed of two-thirds men and one-third women is ideal.** Let as many persons as wish come up on the stage, and don't send any down just because all of the seats are taken. The ones who can't get seats may stand in the rear of the seated group. Having this overflow gives you a natural excuse to send those persons down whom you spot as possible trouble makers, as you explain that obviously you have more subjects than you can possibly use, but that you will give them all an equal chance, and will keep those persons on the stage who concentrate the best. **Then give them all a preliminary group test, and the subjects you do not desire to retain dismiss at once, until you have all of the chairs full of good, potential subjects.**

Judging Your Committee

Observation is the best teacher in spotting your best subjects; it's a knack that comes through experience. But, generally speaking, your good subjects usually have either a serious or nervous, self-conscious demeanor, and sit with both feet on the floor. Usually you can notice a sort of relaxed "look" about them. If the girls sit together in a row they have a tendency to giggle, so separate them in the group, spacing them among the boys. Usually they will then co-operate much better. Subjects you should avoid and dismiss as promptly as is possible are the ones who sit down with a cocky "Now you show me air" and cross their legs, subjects who come up in pairs and insist on talking to each other or other members of the committee; subjects who chew gum and smoke or smell of alcohol should also be gotten rid of as soon as you can diplomatically. And beware of the subject with the perpetual grin. He may not deliberately mean harm, but his smirk can undermine phenomena. **This spotting and judging of good and bad subjects is one of the first things the Stage Hypnotist must learn for the smooth staging of his show.**

Using Plants and Starting the Show

The use of confederates in the audience still has its place to a limited extent in the modern hypnotic act, not as fake subjects to be sure, but in the acting as "starters" for the other subjects. **Be sure you always use genuine hypnotic subjects for these, however.** With two or three plants in your committee you can always feel certain that your critical "example tests" are going to work, which is an important factor in getting the rest of the committee to properly respond. A few hypnotic plants in various parts of the theatre also will assist in acting as "starters" in getting subjects to come forward to the stage so you can start the show without delay. Sometimes there is hesitancy on the part of volunteers to come forward immediately, but once someone starts the parade the others follow willingly enough. This factor of reticence on the part of subjects to come forward must be considered by the practical performer in the staging of his show, as it gets things off to a very bad start to have to coax persons to come up on the stage. A good, enthusiastic bunch of individuals coming forward to the stage at once establishes interest, and the more you get on the stage the more obviously the exhibition is in social approval. In this regard, if you are working with an M.C. or person who can introduce your act, you can often let him get the subjects on the stage for you before the actual show starts. Any difficulty or delays he may have make little difference, but when you once come out, make things really "perk!"

Group Hypnotism

Group hypnosis is very important to the stage operator for the percentage factor in a group of persons locates for him his desirable subjects. Actually, in some ways it is easier to hypnotize many subjects while working with the entire group than it is individually. A group seems to develop a mutual spirit of co-operation that carries from one subject to the other until all are responding in unison. **Your rule in handling group hypnotic phenomena is to make it clearly understood exactly what is expected of the subjects, and give your suggestions clear and loud.** Emphasize your verbal suggestions visually as much as possible. For this reason it is a good policy to often demonstrate the test you intend to work with a single subject before applying it to the group. Seeing the one subject react, the group quickly understands exactly what reaction is expected of them, and the success of the test on the subject sets its success as applied.

Progressive Selling

Although it is rarely expressed in such terms, Stage Hypnotism is actually a sales situation in which you sell the subjects a "bill of goods." Your whole approach is to arrange the show so that each test sells the subjects on responding to the next; thus each test is important to the success of the one that follows, forming a chain reaction that flows through the entire show. **For this reason routine your show so that the beginning, simple experiments lead up gradually toward the more complex.** Properly routined "Progressive Selling" is the answer to the successful hypnotic show.

The High Pressure of Stage Hypnotism

If ever the words "High Pressure Selling" were aptly used it is in describing the techniques of the stage hypnotizer. Every device the performer can muster is thrown in a continuous barrage at the subjects to induce the proper mental conditions for hypnosis. **The "High Pressure" must be artfully applied however, as the more completely it is disguised the more effective the technique.**

Repetition and Clearness of Suggestions

In order for the mind in the hypnotic state to properly assimilate suggestions they must be very clearly given. To that end always repeat your suggestive ideas. **Make it your rule to repeat every suggestion you give at least two times in order that it may be properly assimilated by the subject, and secondly always speak clearly, simply, and directly to the subject, or subjects as the case may be.**

One Thing At a Time

Always remember this basic rule in the giving of hypnotic suggestions to present one idea, or suggestion series, at a time, and after the response to the suggestion has occurred, remove it before further ideas are presented. **This is very important not only to your personal success in hypnotizing but to your subject's well being as well.**

Don't Expect Too Much

In giving suggestions for your subjects to react to, don't give them things too foreign to their natures. Gauge the tests you try with each subject within his capacity. **If you will remember this rule your work will prove far more striking in the production of seemingly brilliant phenomena.**

Use Your Best Subjects

Here is a secret always to be applied. As your act progresses you can invariably spot your most responsive subjects. **Now use these good subjects for your critical, individual tests.** To use a sales analogy again, let these subjects form your "Product" which you demonstrate in the selling of hypnotic powers to the best of the committee.

Trance Depth in Stage Demonstrations

Although it varies, of course, with individuals, in general the depth of trance produced under the rapid techniques of Stage Hypnotism is not as deep as that developed by the slower, more methodical methods of the psychological laboratory. This makes little difference to the performer, except that it must be considered in the handling of his subjects. **Make it your rule to have your tests as easy for your subject to perform as is possible.** From the audience's point-of-view the test produced through light trance such as muscular catalepsies are every bit as effective as are the more advanced experiments. So until you are certain of your subject's trance depth don't expect too much of him and your initial experiments gauged to lighter trance levels.

Keeping the Subject Entranced

The stage methods of hypnotizing are so rapid and high-pressure in nature that they tend to be somewhat unstable, so unless pressure is maintained to carry the subject along with it, the subject is apt to slip spontaneously out of the trance if left too long by himself. **For the most part then, keep your subjects active and busy responding to a flow of suggestions; then awaken**

them between tests rather than just leaving them sleeping. It is important, too, to give sleep retaining suggestions at intervals, such as, "Nothing will awaken you until I count to five. You are going down deeper and deeper to sleep continuously with every breath you take. Everything you do will send you deeper to sleep. No one can awaken you or even disturb you except myself, etc." Such suggestions tend to overcome the tendency of stage subjects to awaken of their own accord.

Simulation

Considerable numbers of subjects, especially in the extravert enterprise of performing on the stage, tend to simulate hypnosis rather than actually going completely into the trance. This simulation is not necessarily voluntary deception, for it is frequently born of an extreme desire to co-operate with the performer and help out the show, and yet, not having the innate mental make-up for entering true somnambulism, the subject does his very best to imitate the genuine condition. This is a factor very vital to the performer and it greatly increases the number of entertaining subjects that he has to work with. He should, however, be able to pick the genuine from the false, though, in order to properly select his subjects for the various tests. This takes a practiced eye, and need not be of too great a concern for you, as the precise mental condition of the subject is not too important so long as the outward appearance of the subject is correct. For on the stage, the show is the thing, and as long as the audience is satisfied you can also afford to be.

Deliberate Faking

It is a far cry from the unconsciously simulating subject trying to do his best for the success of the show to the subject who deliberately pretends to be hypnotized just to fool you. The former is usually in a half-trance anyway, and in many cases the simulation will shortly pass on to complete hypnosis. **But the latter is dangerous!** So keep a wary eye out for such pranksters as they greatly harm your show. Such subjects have a habit of pretending to be asleep while you are watching them, and then while your back is turned open their eyes and poke fun at you, and then seemingly return to sleep before you can spot them. **Whenever a laugh comes in your show for no apparent reason, be on your guard that someone is faking, and spot that trouble-maker as soon as possible, and once you do locate him, get him off the stage immediately.** If he refuses to go, be as undiplomatic as you like in picking him up by the coat collar and unceremoniously leading him back to his seat. You will find that the audience will credit you for thus disposing of a disturbing influence. A way to catch these fakes is to occasionally unexpectedly, turn around, or have someone stationed in the wings who watches the subjects constantly, and if he sees that a subject is faking, hold up the number of fingers representing the chair number in which the subject is seated.

Every Magician knows that it is in the attention to details that the mediocre becomes great, so, too, it is with Hypnotism.

HYPNOTISM AS ENTERTAINMENT

The majority of medical and academic students of Hypnotism are largely against stage exhibitions of Hypnotism. While such need be of little concern to the Magician, any such prejudice from the public, itself, can be hurtful. Some few towns even have ordinances associating Hypnotists with quacks in general and forbidding hypnotic shows. Now such reactions are all hangovers from a period several decades back when Hypnotists went wild and ran a golden age of box-office successes into the mud of charlatanry. Fortunately, thanks to contemporary research, the subject is currently on a rising wave of esteem, but the modern Magician performing a hypnotic show still has something of an obligation to help in reestablishing the practice to unified popular favor.

The New Stage Hypnotism

The idea behind the old-time hypnotic show was to establish the performer as a sort of master-mind who dominated the wills of all he approached, and to prove his great "powers" he had his "victims" perform all manner of ridiculous experiments. Thus the theme of the show was to heap supposed glory on the performer and ridicule on the subjects.

The modern approach to the hypnotic entertainment is very different from the above, it now being the aim of the performer to heap glory on the phenomenon, itself, and his subjects' ability to react to it. The Hypnotist, himself, assumes the modest role of guide. There is sound psychology in such an approach that completely revolutionizes the hypnotic show from its antiquated predecessor; modernizes it to meet present-day demands, vindicates Hypnotism from prejudice, and lifts it to the height of Art.

The Presentation of Stage Hypnotism

Every performer has his own style of working, thus some Magicians will hypnotize with smooth persuasive techniques, while other will utilize more aggressive methods. And the routines too, and the variety of effects presented will vary with the individual performer . . . but underlying the entire presentation of your hypnotic act always incorporate these six basic rules:

Rule No. 1. **Never clown.** Hypnotism from your viewpoint as the performer must always be essentially a serious business. This does not mean that you are to be glum in your presentation. In fact, be lively and dynamic. But deliberate jokes have no place in the presentation of Stage Hypnotism. Let all of your humor come from the subject matter itself.

Rule No. 2. **Never ridicule your subjects.** Remember, your committee is composed of volunteers from the audience itself, and to ridicule them is the same as ridiculing your audience . . . which is entertainment suicide. Always treat your subjects with the utmost in courtesy and respect. While some of your effects may be extremely funny, always make them serve the end in your presentation of illustrating some hypnotic principle; not to make the subjects appear ridiculous.

Rule No. 3. **Incorporate science in your presentation.** The exact degree to which you can do this depends upon your personality as an entertainer and the type of audiences to which you play. But always, to some extent keep a background of scientific experimentation in your hypnotic work.

Rule No. 4. **Take your audience honestly into your confidence.** Hypnotism has long enough been shrouded in mystery, and even as a Magician you will find that plenty still exists, so you can well afford to frankly discuss its phenomenon and remove the veil from its secrets. For example, don't be afraid to place the credit for hypnotic occurrences where it belongs—to the minds of the subjects themselves. Don't be afraid to admit that you have no especial powers over the minds of your subjects. Don't be afraid to explain that the underlying principles of Hypnotism are simply the working of psychological law without a vestige of the supernatural. You will find that such honest frankness far from destroying your prestige in the eyes of the

audience will elevate it immensely. People nowadays like to consider themselves intellectual enough to consider scientfic problems, and facts of science about the working of their own minds have a tremendous fascination. As for reducing the mystery; do you reduce the mystery of electricity by explaining some of things it can do? Conversely, you only increase its wonders. So it is with Hypnotism. The more you explain of its wonders, the deeper the wonder you produce.

Rule No. 5. **Interest your committee.** As a Hypnotist you have one factor completely foreign to the presentation of the Magician; all of your props are human. You must therefore hold the interest of those "props" (your subjects) with forceful completeness. To such ends your presentation as a Hypnotist becomes a dual process that must include your committee as well as your audience.

Rule No. 6. **Always Entertain.** Always remember that your foremost purpose as a stage performer is to entertain. It is so easy to become so wrapped up in subject matter as Hypnotism offers that you seek to perform tests that entertain yourself but hold little meaning to the audience as a whole. Make everything you do convey a message and have a purpose. Make every effect you show have entertainment value. No matter how intellectual and scientfic your hypnotic show may be, remember its value to theatrical audiences is nil unless it is also entertaining.

Your thorough mystery of hypnotic technique, your development of a smoothly routined hypnotic show, your incorporation of these six rules spell **Success** in the presentation of Stage Hypnotism.

Combining Magic with Hypnotism

On first thought it might seem that the combining of magical effects to the hypnotic show might raise doubts as to the authenticity of the Hypnotism. Experience proves such not the case, however, for in the public's mind the tricks of the Magician are taken as a matter-of-course as an innate part of his art, in no sense a form of deception. Actually Magic and Hypnotism blend beautifully together to form exciting entertainment.

For example if you are working a full evening show, a first act of Magic and a second act of Hypnotism offers a well-balanced mystery program that is decidedly hard to beat. And you will find that having first established yourself as a first-class Magician will so raise your prestige that hypnotizing becomes just that much the easier.

For the shorter show likewise Magic fits in nicely with Hypnotism; the show starting out with a series of magical effects and then proceeding to the hypnotic experiments. An opening line such as, "This evening I will show you examples of the two basic types of Magic —the Magic of the Magician and the Magic of the human mind, commonly called Hypnotism. Let us begin first with an effect of the conjuror," ties them neatly together. **And be sure to have your last Magic effect just prior to the Hypnotism one that will thoroughly mystify the audience and leave them in admiration of your skill.**

It is also well to have a group of tricks all ready to go in the event that you run into difficulty in presenting the hypnotic part of your program. This can be a great comfort, knowing that you have something to fall back on in an emergency. With such a safe-guard the Magician need never have the slightest worry about the results of his hypnotic show. If everything goes perfectly, fine, but if the committee should prove refractory then he can simply slide gracefully into his Magic with some remark as, "Thus you have seen a few examples of the Magic of the human mind. Now for my next effect, etc.," and continue right on using members of the committee in some magical effect. The audience will never know that your hypnotic results were not exactly what you intended, for as in Magic you never explain what you are going to do until you do it.

Creating New Effects

Now that you know the how of Hypnotism and the types of phenomena that you can produce, the variety of effects and combinations of effects you can create are almost infinite. It is in this creative phase of developing your hypnotic show that you can show your individualism and originality. By way of illustrating the prospect for developing new effects, let us consider a test in post-hypnotic negative hallucination.

The first experiment we will call "The Invisible Performer."

Hypnotize your subject and give him the suggestions that when he awakens he will be perfectly normal in all ways, except that he will not be able to see you. He will be able to see everyone and everything else, and even able to hear and feel you, but that you will be absolutely invisible to him, until such time as you snap your fingers beside his ear. Then awaken him.

The reaction you can imagine as he looks vainly about trying to find you, his surprise at hearing your voice or feeling your touch while you are invisible, and then the climax when you suddenly materialize before his eyes at the snap of your fingers. Now for the second experiment, which we will call, "The Dancing Handkerchief."

Hypnotize your subject and give him the suggestions that when he awakens he will be perfectly normal in all ways, but that he will see a handkerchief dancing about the stage entirely under its own power. And that, look as closely as he will, he will not see any person or anything holding up the handkerchief and moving it about. That handkerchief will seem to be dancing about all by itself. Then waken the subject and let someone take the handkerchief by the corner and dance it about the stage. A strange thing will happen, the moment the person takes hold of the corner of the handkerchief he disappears to the subject and the handkerchief seemingly becomes motivated by itself.

In the above you will observe how we have an identical hypnotic condition, yet the effect from the audience's point-of-view is very different indeed. Thought and ingenuity on your part to the creating of new effects can make the production aspects of your show as completely original as you can possibly desire.

Make Your Phenomena Visual

Directly in line with this developing of effects is the caution to be sure to make your effects visual to the audience. No matter how profound the hypnosis you induce, there would be little entertainment value in observing a subject witnessing an hallucination unless he responds to that hallucination with action. For example, what a contrast we have in audience enjoyment if we say to the subject, "When you open your eyes you will see a cat on the floor" to our saying, "When you open your eyes you will see a cat on the floor, it will rub itself against your leg. You will love that cat, you will pick it up and play with it. Then it will suddenly get angry and try to scratch you, and you will throw it from you." In the former the subject merely sits looking blankly at the floor with an introspective stare. To be sure he sees the hallucination, but the audience cannot be expected to see within his mind. While in the latter test the whole procedure is so graphic that the entertaining pantomime leaves nothing to be desired. **Remember to make it your rule to establish in all of your hypnotic tests an action response so that the audience can visually follow the experiment and be entertained by its effect.**

Emphasize Your Effects

You can also greatly increase the entertainment value of your effects if you will amplify the subject's reactions by your showmanship in exhibiting those reactions. By way of illustration, let's suppose that you have suggested to a subject that when he awakens from the trance that he will find himself blind, and that he will grope his way about the stage unable to see a single thing until you tell him that his sight will return. You can easily realize how such an effect can be amplified by having other members of the committee wave their hands in front of the "blinded" eyes of the subject, or by you having him stand with his eyes wide open, staring directly out into the audience as you pass a lighted match back and forth in front of his eyes, while the audience looks on in breathless horror at the unwavering stare. Of such devices the showmanship of Hypnotism is made.

Speed and Time in the Hypnotic Show

Every device you can muster to add to the pace of your hypnotic show will increase its entertainment value, and to such ends first and foremost utilize the principle of post-hypnosis by invariably suggesting at the end of each trance just before you awaken the subject that the next time you attempt to hypnotize the subject that he will go instantly to sleep. You can thus increase tremendously the speed with which you work.

And give consideration to the length of your over-all show. Hypnotism offers such a tremendous scope of emotions that too much of it at one time can rather exhaust an audience. Keep yourself alert in watching your audience's reaction, and when you feel that your audience might be in danger of becoming saturated with phenomena, always wind up your show. A show of an hour's length is usually ample for Hypnotism. While it is true that a full evening's program of two hours or more have been given, you will find that your program will hold much more entertainment appeal if you balance the hypnotic part with other related types of entertainment, such as Magic or mind-reading effects. **Make it your rule, more strongly in the hyp-**

notic program than in any other type, to always leave your audience wanting more! Conversely, don't make your hypnotic program too short. It is doubtful if a good, convincing demonstration of Hypnotism can be given in less than twenty minutes.

The Skeleton of the Hypnotic Entertainment

No matter what precise effects you use or what the length of your show, the modern hypnotic program invariably follows a certain pattern. So use this skeleton in developing your own hypnotic show:

INTRODUCTION
OPENING LECTURE
COMMITTEE INVITATION
FIRST TEST WITH ENTIRE GROUP
EXPERIMENTS IN WAKING SUGGESTION
INDIVIDUAL EXAMPLE OF HYPNOTISM
GROUP HYPNOSIS
EXPERIMENTS IN HYPNOTIC SUGGESTION
COMMITTEE DISMISSAL
CONCLUSION

The exact length of time and the exact effects you will give to each section of that "skeleton" depends entirely upon the exact show you are preparing. But for your hypnotic show to be entirely successful and acceptable always construct it in the above sequence.

To sum up, Hypnotism as entertainment is essentially a show that reveals the hypnotic mysteries of the human mind through graphic experiments, humorous incidents, scientific explanations, and thought-provoking phenomena.

Of such is the entertainment of modern Stage Hypnotism.

HYPNOTIC STAGECRAFT

Having mastered all of the intricacies of your hypnotic show, the last step is how will you stage it. And a most important step it is . . . for this is the package in which you sell your product.

While the hypnotic show can possibly be staged more simply than almost any other type of entertainment, with no more ado than a group of chairs on the stage, such is no reason why the progressive performer should be thus easily satisfied. In this chapter we shall, therefore, give the variety of devices with which the Stage Hypnotist can colorfully cloak his art.

The Chairs

When the curtain goes up the first thing the audience sees is a group of chairs on the stage. These are your props as a Hypnotist and function exactly as do magic tables to the Magician. As such it logically follows that the nicer the appearance of these chairs the nicer the appearance of your stage setting. A straggly group of chairs of a variety of types, sizes and colors is quite a contrast to a neat and orderly row of identical chairs. Then, too, you are shortly to invite volunteers to come forward and sit in those chairs, so it is important to have them look inviting to the potential committee.

The exact type of chair you use is immaterial, but an armless, straight-back type is best as you can get more on the stage without crowding. Folding chairs strong. And have all of your chairs uniform in type, are fine, but be sure they are in good condition and size, and color. While usually the chairs are obtained from the place where the show is being given, if the performer really wishes to stage his show in ultra fashion, what could be neater than a row of chrome-plated folding chairs with a black seat and back rest. Whatever the chairs you use, keep your purpose to have them look trim and neat (See Fig. 74), and have rubber "stops" on each leg so that they won't slide.

FIG. 74

Arrange your chairs in a semi-circle on the stage starting near the first wing on each side of the stage (See Fig. 75), and place them about eight inches apart, so that while the subjects will be seated closely together, they will not touch each other. Figure twenty-five chairs as the maximum number of chairs you will need and fifteen as your minimum. Around twenty chairs is the average number you will use.

It is important not to use too few chairs, as the more persons you have on the stage, the more potential subjects you have to work with. Also the larger the group, the more important the experiments seem to the audience, and the subjects gain confidence by

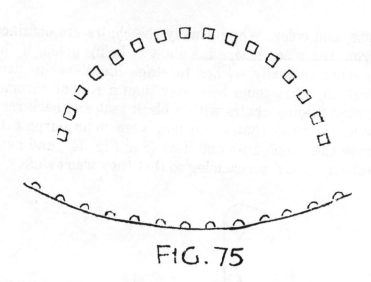

FIG. 75

being in a large group. You will find there is a mass action in committee size that makes it easier to hypnotize when you have a large number of persons on the stage. You can also get volunteers to come up more readily if they see they are going to be in a crowd rather than spotted out individually.

It is well, in addition to the group of committee chairs, to have one **special chair** that you set apart and use for the individual tests. This chair can be larger in size and more comfortable. Make it seem as though when sitting in that special chair that something especial is likely to happen. While it is not really essential, two devices can be applied to that chair that will increase your subject's responsiveness; No. 1: To wire the arms of the chair so that a tingling electric current passes into the palms of the subject's hands as he sits in it. This can be easily rigged by having the cushions on the chair arms slightly damp, and wired to the electric power off stage. Don't use enough current to disturb the subject, just enough to produce a mild tingling. **Remember, the effect you want is psychologi-**

cal anticipation, not an electrical shock, so have an electrician rig it for you correctly. (See Fig. 76).

FIG. 76

No. 2 is to cut off about a quarter to a half-inch from one of the rear legs of the chair (See Fig. 77).

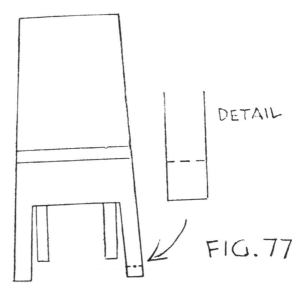

DETAIL

FIG. 77

This throws it just enough out of line so as to make the seat seem a bit unsteady. This slight eccentricity in the "feel" of the chair adds just enough to the mental anxiety in the subject's mind as he faces the prospect of being hypnotized as to frequently produce immediate hypnosis. Also, when the subject's eyes are closed and you stand behind him, you can rock the chair slightly to emphasize your suggestions of sinking and floating away down to deep, deep sleep.

The Curtains

Most performers will make use of whatever curtains they find on the stages on which they perform, but if you have any choice in the matter, or intend to get a curtain of your own to hang, get one of a deep color. Black, blue or rich wine are fine, the essential thing in color being that it will contrast well with your subjects on the stage and make their actions stand out. In this regard also, if you have a design on the curtain keep it simple so as not to distract from stage action, and leave a good portion of the curtain just plain. If you decide to use a designed drop, have something that builds up your prestige such as your name in glittering letters (See Fig. 78), or else make it atmospheric with hypnotic eyes peering forth, or some such (See 79). The important thing in selecting a curtain is to have

FIG. 78

it designed to fit the type of act you are presenting to form a picture-like setting for the variety of thing you do.

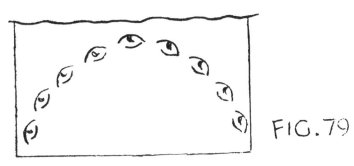

FIG. 79

The Lights

Generally speaking the lighting of a hypnotic show should be routined along the following lines:

For your Introduction and Opening Remarks have your stage lights on **Reds** and **Blues**, and work in a **White Spot.**

As you invite the subjects up on the stage, bring your stage lights **full up** and turn on the **house lights** as well. Once your subjects are seated on the stage **turn out the house lights, but leave stage lights full up for your first group test.**

From here on through the show, your light pattern is **Stage Reds** and **Blues** for each test with a single subject, and **full up** for all group tests. **Give your spot-light man instructions to follow you with a White Spot at all times.**

Below are a number of special lighting effects that can add variety to your show:

Have a baby spot mounted overhead in the grids. Have an amber gelatine over the lens and focus it vertically downward directly at your special hypnotic chair near stage center (See Fig. 80).

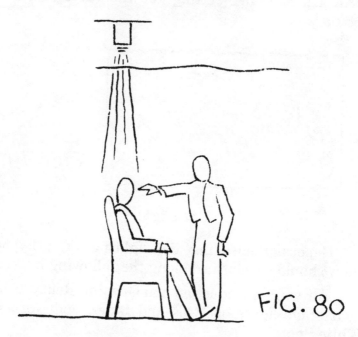

FIG. 80

A baby spot in the wings focused at the performer face is also very effective. Try it with a green gelatine (See Fig. 81).

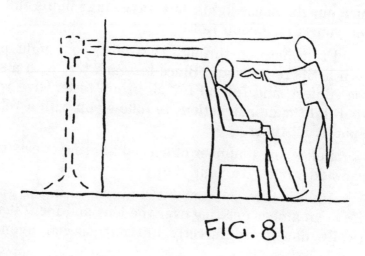

FIG. 81

In the event that you cannot conveniently arrange for such a baby spot, a floor lamp placed behind the subject's chair and directed over his shoulder towards the performer will give an interesting, informal lighting effect (See Fig. 82).

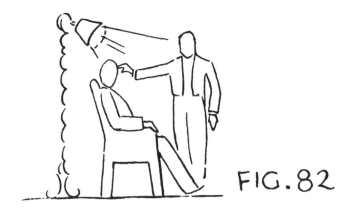

FIG. 82

A double-faced mirror mounted upright on a revolving turntable with a spot focused on it gives a most hypnotic effect as it revolves (See Fig. 83). Place this device behind the first curtain wing, and as it revolves the mirrors reflect out flashes of light about the stage (See Fig. 84). This is especially effective to use while hypnotizing a solo subject.

FIG. 83

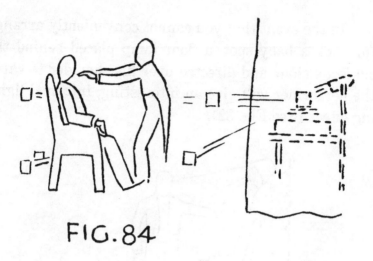

FIG. 84

Hang a revolving globe covered with small pieces of mirror overhead, at stage center, and focus a light on it. As it slowly revolves, light flashes are sent throughout the entire theatre producing a very spectacular effect (See Fig. 85). This machine is especially effective to use while hypnotizing the entire committee. Devices such as these enrich the hypnotic show, make it more spectacular, and take the hypnotic effects over the footlights right to the spectators themselves.

Colored lights have definite psychological affects on hypnotic subjects, so remember these principles and use them in staging your hypnotic show:

Yellow light increases the subject's suggestibility, while Purple, Blue, and Green light are sleep inducing. You can apply these affects to your stage hypnotism techniques by arranging a lamp with two bulbs placed so it will shine directly at the face of the subject (See Fig. 86). When you first commence to hypnotize switch on the **Yellow light.** Then as his eyes close and you follow on into the "sleep formula" switch off the yellow and turn on the **Purple light.** You will find the use of these colored lights a very spectacular and effective way to hypnotize your subjects.

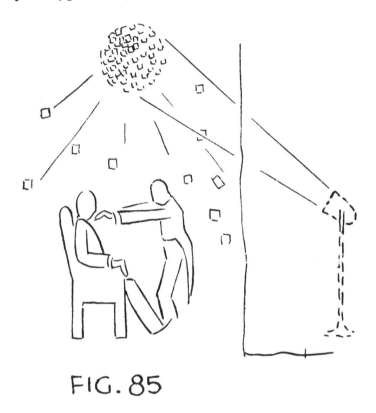

FIG. 85

The Mike

The use of a Public Address System is absolutely essential to the modern hypnotic show, and the mike forms the very heart of your performing. When the curtain first goes up, there it is in the center of the stage ready for use in your introduction, opening lecture, and for use throughout your entire show. And take that mike with you as you perform your different tests. Your audience will thus be able to follow your suggestions and clearly understand exactly what is going on at all times.

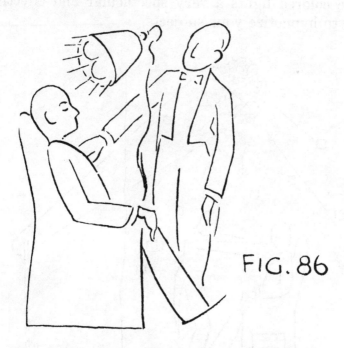

FIG. 86

The mike is important also in making your voice more commanding. Especially when working with the entire committee as a group is this vital, as everyone of your subjects through the P.A. speakers can thus clearly hear you. **The use of the microphone is your secret for holding the attention of your subjects and your audience at one and the same time.**

If you prefer, a lapel mike may be used. This has the advantage of being small and portable as you move about the stage, but you must be careful not to become tangled in the wire. If your P.A. System has "inputs" for two mikes one in the center and one at the side of the stage is very convenient.

The Music

Musical background is extremely important to the success of the hypnotic show. If you have an orchestra or organist with which to work you can get some wonderful effects, but for most shows the use of records played over the P.A. System works out splendidly.

The essential thing in selecting hypnotic music is to use pieces that are not too well known and that are soothing rather than arousing. Organ or symphonic are usually best. Get pieces that suggest sleep, dreams, or a mood of quiet and rest . . . and make certain the piece keeps the same sound level throughout with no sudden changes. Having selected the music you like, apply it to these spots in your show:

BEFORE THE SHOW (Use a dramatic symphonic selection.)

AS SUBJECTS COME TO STAGE (Use a smooth selection with a bit of lively rhythm in it to encourage them in coming to the stage.)

FIRST HYPNOTIC MOOD TEST ON ENTIRE COMMITTEE (Use soft, dreamy, hypnotic music. **Music in this spot is a must for every show.**)

HYPNOTIZING THE ENTIRE COMMITTEE (Use soft, dreamy, hypnotic music.)

The exact insertion of music to his effects is up to the individual performer. But the above gives the four essential spots where it must be used. You will find that the use of music definitely increases your control over your subjects and makes it much easier to hypnotize them. Always keep the volume down so the music forms a soft melodious background to your suggestions.

Stage Accessories

These constitute those extra props needed in working the show. A table or two, lemon, glass, pitcher of water, and the various small props you use for the different hypnotic effects. Keep your table well over to the side of the stage so as to be completely out of the way, yet handy so that you can secure what you need quickly.

Assistants

Although the hypnotic show can be very effectively handled on a strictly one-man basis, if you do have assistants they can increase the show's production value. If your male assistant has a good voice he can introduce you and invite the subject on the stage for you. Your girl assistants can bring in the various props as you wish to use them, and can usher the volunteers to their seats as they come to the stage. At the most don't use more than one boy and two girl assistants, and for the most part keep them very inconspicuously in the background.

The Dress

The Hypnotist presenting a formal stage hypnotic show should always wear **"tails."** For programs of a lecture type a neat, double-breasted business suit will work perfectly. You know how good clothes increase prestige, and in Hypnotism prestige is the thing.

If you have assistants, have the boy wear a tuxedo and the girls either evening gowns or nurse's uniforms. Flashy and revealing theatrical costumes are taboo in the hypnotic show. Dignity must be your motif.

Tricks-of-the-Trade

Magnetizing Your Fingertips: Whether or not you give credence to magnetic theories, it is a good idea to stand erect and imagine that you are charging your hands with "force" just before you walk out on the stage at the start of your show. To do this, tense up your fingers, turn your hands palms towards each other, hold them with the fingertips about two inches apart, and imagine or visualize in your mind that an electric-like current is passing down your arms and is flowing out of your fingertips (See Fig. 87). As you practice this you will actually experience a tingling sensation in your fingers. **Get this sensation going strong,** then walk out briskly and start the show.

FIG. 87

The Hypnotic Gaze: For a mysterious gaze in hypnotizing your subject, focus your eyes at a point on the level of his eyes about six inches in back of his head (See Fig. 88). This gives the appearance that each of your eyes is staring directly into his, looking within his very brain, and is very effective in holding attention.

FIG. 88

The Magnetic Bowl of Water: Have on a table near the side of the stage an Oriental type of bowl containing water. Every so often during your show, between effects, go over and dip your hands in the water and then shake them vigorously dry. Believers in the magnetic theory say this helps remove the used magnetism and recharges the hands with fresh vital force. Whatever the reason, it is effective showmanship. **Don't comment about it to your audience or committee. Just do it, and let them wonder as they will.**

Perfumes and Incense: Odors have their place in the hypnotic show. Have your girl assistants wear potent, Oriental smelling perfumes. And a pot or two of incense burning on each side of the stage has its purpose. Devices such as this that lend atmosphere to the hypnotic show, are all effective and increase the anticipation of both the committee members and the audience for miracles to come.

Challenge Hypnotism: Some of the more bombastic performers, who deliberately issue challenges to hypnotize any person, have made use of such concealing odors as perfumes and incense, on the stage, to make it possible to apply this subtle method of hypnotizing difficult subjects. First rig up this device; get a small bottle, drill two holes in a rubber cork and insert in the hole a couple of short lengths of glass tubing so that they project about a half an inch on each side of the cork. Next place some anaesthetic chloroform in the bottle and cork tightly. Get a length of rubber tubing with a bulb attached and fasten it to one of the projecting glass tubes. This bulb has a one-way valve in it so that on squeezing air will be forced into the bottle. To the other glass tube fasten another length of rubber tubing (See Fig. 89).

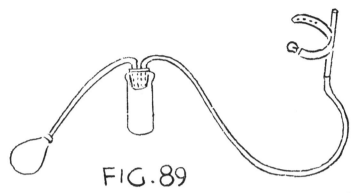

FIG. 89

Now adjust the apparatus to your person by placing the bottle in your right hip pocket, the bulb in your left trouser pocket, and run the long tube down the inside of your right coat sleeve. The exact length of these tubes will depend upon your build, of course. Insert a length of glass tubing in the end of the long rubber tube, and arrange a wrist band so you can strap it securely in place to the inside of your right wrist. The overall length of this tube should terminate just within your coat sleeve (See Fig. 90).

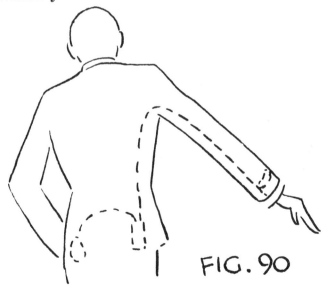

FIG. 90

In hypnotizing with this apparatus, place a pot of burning incense on the floor near your subject so the smoke will rise up towards his nose, explaining that you will now apply an Oriental method of hypnosis to his case. Then proceed to hypnotize him by your favorite method. After his eyes are closed, begin giving suggestions of sleep, and combined with the suggest that the odor from the incense is beginning to change and is getting stronger and more potent, and that it is sending him down deep, deep into sleep. Continuing with such suggestions, keep squeezing the bulb in your pocket, and as your right hand makes passes over the front of his face the chloroform vapor goes directly to his nostrils (See Fig. 91).

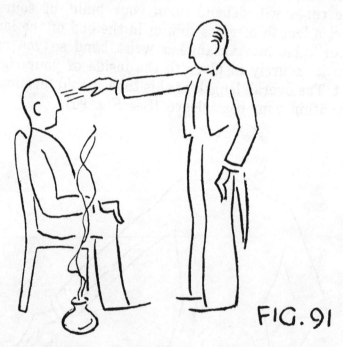

FIG. 91

Needless to say your use of chloroform must be kept a strict secret, and that is the purpose of the incense, as its odor combined with your suggestions of odd odors sending him down to sleep covers it to the subject, and the perfumes on stage and the burning incense covers it to the committee and the audience.

You will find this method will greatly assist you in hypnotizing the most stubborn cases, and the trance induced will be genuine hypnosis, as not enough chloroform is given to anaesthetize the subject . . . it merely intensifies the effects of your suggestions, and gets the subject over that "hump" into complete trance.

One last word of warning in using this device, be sure that the glass tubes within the bottle do not touch the liquid; all you wish to do is send the gas of the chloroform towards your subject, not drench him with the liquid.

Associate Mysteries

Hypnotizing Flowers: Use the identical apparatus employed in the previous Challenge Hypnotism Method, and as you wave your hand over a vase of flowers press on the bulb . . . **and the flowers will quickly droop and "go to sleep"** (See 92). It is a very

FIG. 92

little known fact that flowers, too, are susceptible to an anaesthetic. A test of this nature will produce a great deal of comment when seriously associated in your lecture on possible theories of Hypnotism.

Hypnotizing Animals: Small animals such as mice and birds can likewise be put to sleep by an application of the anaesthetizing apparatus as used in the "Flower Test," but there are other methods of influencing them likewise that are "naturals" for the Stage Hypnotist. While the hypnosis induced by these methods are no true hypnotism in the strict sense of the term, the effects of the tests are all that could be desired for audience presentation.

To hypnotize a **Frog** or a **Lizard,** flop it over on its back and hold it immobile for a few seconds. Then carefully remove your hands, and the animal will remain exactly as you left it—sleeping (See Fig 93). To remove the condition, snap your fingers for effect, and quickly flop it over right side up.

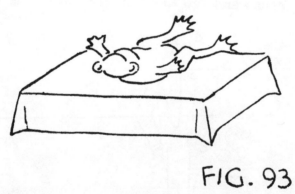

FIG. 93

To hypnotize a **Lobster,** stand it up on its head, using its claws as supports (See Fig. 94). Hold it thus for a few moments, and it will go instantly to sleep. To remove the condition merely set it again on its legs.

FIG. 94

To hypnotize a **Chicken,** catch hold of the bird by its neck, and force the hen's head down so it lies flat to the ground. Then with a piece of chalk draw a line directly out from its beak for about two feet (See Fig. 95). Then carefully remove your hands and it will stay in that exact position motionless. To awaken, clap your hands loudly beside it, and push its head a bit away from the chalk line.

FIG. 95

To hypnotize a **Guinea Pig,** first roll the animal over and over a few times on your table, and then lay it on its back (See Fig. 96). The guinea pig will remain quiescent until you blow on its nose and return it to its feet.

FIG. 96

To hypnotize a **Rabbit,** lay it on its back, part its ears with the fingers of your right hand flat on the table, and push its hind legs down to the table with your left hand (See Fig. 97). Hold the animal thus stretched out on its back, restricting its movements for about thirty seconds, and then carefully remove your hands. The rabbit will lie outstretched on its back —hypnotized. To remove the influence, blow sharply on its nose, and push it over on its side. It will immediately awaken and scamper about.

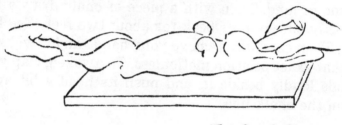

FIG. 97

The Taste Test: This charlatan test makes use of a simply-made piece of equipment. Get a small rubber ball. Make a hole in its side, and in this hole glue tightly one end of a piece of small rubber tubing. Have this tubing of such a length as to reach from under your right arm-pit to your wrist. Now make another small hole in the ball, and drop in a few grains of **powdered sacchrine.** Seal up the hole with a bit of adhesive tape and tie the tube so the ball will rest under your right arm pit, and run the tube down your sleeve, fastening the lower end of the tube to the inside of your wrist with a rubber band just within the edge of the coat sleeve (See Fig. 98).

So prepared, hold up a candy bar and ask each person to imagine how it would taste, as you continue giving suggestions of a sweet taste coming into their

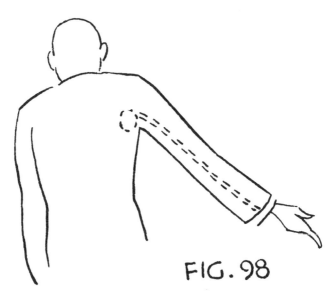

FIG. 98

mouths. As you give these suggestions, pass rapidly down the row of your committee, waving your right hand in front of the face of each subject, and as you pass the subject's mouth press your arm sharply against your side. This forces a tiny spray of the powdered sacchrine from out of your sleeve, directly toward the mouth of the subject. The spray is so fine that it is entirely invisible, but the sacchrine is so concentrated in its sweetness, that every subject must confess that he does indeed experience a very real sweetness in response to your "suggestions." Experiments of this nature which employ artifices to emphasize your suggestions can be very useful in establishing beyond a shadow of a doubt the reality of your phenomena. You will find them especially valuable to utilize toward the beginning of your show.

Chevreul's Pendulum: This device, which you can very easily construct by merely tying a finger ring to a length of thread you will find very useful in your stage demonstrations to clearly illustrate the power of suggestion.

Have the subject hold the string between the thumb and forefinger of his right hand, and let the ring dangle free (See Fig. 99). Have him hold the ring just as still as he can, and then suggest that he think to himself of it commencing to swing from right to left back and forth. Keep repeating the idea of it swinging back and forth over and over, and in a few moments the ring will actually commence swinging back and forth, back and forth.

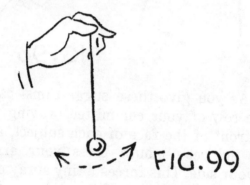

FIG. 99

Now, have your subject change his thought to the idea of the ring commencing to swing around and around in a circle. In direct response to that thought, the ring will stop its back and forth path, and will swing in a wide circle.

As a stage demonstration, each person in the committee can be given a Pendulum and all work it together as a group.

Hypnotizing with Mechancal Devices

These devices will prove very effective in stage demonstrations of Hypnotism. They capture the imagination of the spectators making it both easier for the performer to hypnotize and add spectacle to his show.

With a Flashlight—The After-Image Technique:
My friend, Charles Cook, developed an interesting
method of hypnotizing employing a simple mechani-
cal device—**a pocket Penlite.**

In this technique the subject is seated facing you
in readiness for hypnosis. Suddenly you lean forward,
place the palm of your left hand over his right eye and
shine the Penlite directly into his left eye, holding the
light about an inch from the eye (See Fig. 100). Tell
the subject to keep staring into the light, and to relax
his body completely. After about thirty seconds command him to close his eyes tightly together. Thanks to
the flash light previously directed in his eye he will
now experience a very vivid after-image, and this sensation you describe to him applying it thus: "You will

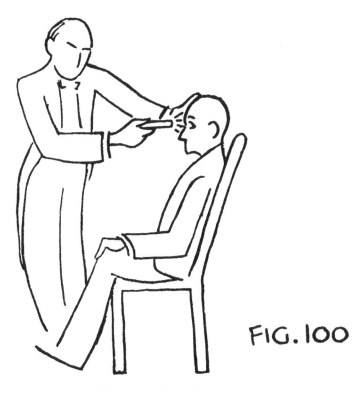

FIG. 100

see inside of your closed lids a very bright spot of light. This spot will change in color and size as you watch it. It will fade away altogether, and then it will reappear. Watch closely this spot, and as you watch it you will begin to feel yourself getting very drowsy and sleepy. Watch it and go to sleep, etc." Continue on with the process to hypnotize your subject. **The principle of this ingenious method is to use the after-image in the subject's own eye as the "fixation object" rather than an external point.** You will find the method highly effective.

The Hindu Hypnograph Buttons: These you prepare yourself or have an artist prepare for you. Trace the outline and design of the buttons (Fig. 101) on a piece of cardboard and fill in the black portions with black drawing ink. Then cut around the outline of each and you have a number of small disks or buttons. Have enough of them so that you can give one to each of your subjects. (These buttons printed on stiff white cardboard may also be obtained from the publishers of this book.)

FIG. 101

When you have distributed the Hypnograph Buttons, have your subjects hold them up in front of their eyes and center their gaze on the little white dot (See

Fig. 102). Using these as your "fixation object" proceed to hypnotize, giving suggestions of the **Disc** becoming blurred before the subject's eyes, that his eyelids are getting heavy, etc., and then when the eyes close that his hand holding up the Disc is becoming heavy and is falling to his lap. When his hand falls, proceed into your "sleep formula" inducing complete hypnosis. This is a very good stage method to use when first hypnotizing your entire group of subjects at one and the same time.

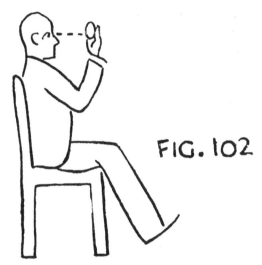

FIG. 102

The Hypnotic Spiral: Here is one of the most effective machines that has yet been developed for producing hypnosis on a whole audience. The machine is very simple to make; simply design a black and white twelve-inch spiral disc, and mount this disc on a phonograph turntable. Then set the device up vertically directly facing towards the audience. Start the motor and note the highly compelling hypnotic effect it produces as it revolves. In designing your disc your rule is, the larger your audience the coarser the lines you use in drawing the spiral (See Fig. 103).

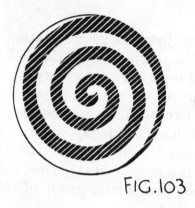

FIG. 103

In using The Hypnotic Spiral, apply your technique of audience hypnosis, but rather than have the spectators gaze toward your eyes, have them center their attention upon the center of the revolving spiral disc. For mass Hypnotism you will find this machine more attention compelling than using just your eyes, and with it large numbers of spectators can be hypnotized. (See Fig. 104).

FIG. 104

The Hypnotic Spiral For Individual Hypnosis: For this purpose design another twelve-inch black and white spiral disc (See Fig. 105). Mount the disc on the turntable arranged on a stand so it can be elevated and placed above the eye level of your subject (See Fig. 106). Set the disc about six inches from the eyes

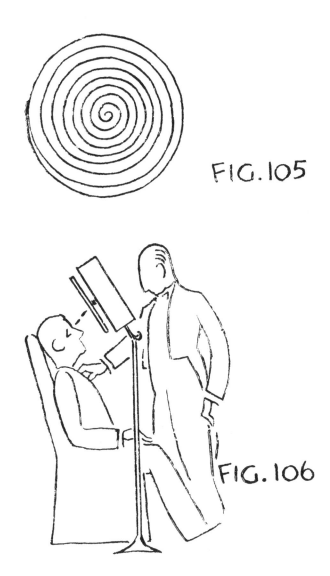

FIG. 105

FIG. 106

of the subject, and instruct him to stare at the center of the disc as long as he can keep his eyes open. Then start the disc rotating and apply your favorite hypnotic method. The hypnotic effect of this machine is extremely powerful and will hypnotize rapidly many of the most difficult subjects.

Again I am indebted to the ingenuity of Mr. Charles Cook for these remarkable spiral hypnotic machines.

The Hypnotic Mirror: This device is illustrated in Fig. 83, and set up in the center of the stage it forms a very good machine with which to induce mass hypnosis. Be sure to adjust the spot light to reflect properly so that the light flashes will reach every spectator as the mirrors revolve, and use a turntable motor with a speed regulator so you can time the flashes correctly. Practice will give you the exact rhythm to use. This is very important as too rapid or too slow a revolution will not give the desired hypnotic effect. You can best secure the correct rate of flash speed by seating yourself in the audience prior to the show and having your assistant vary the motor speed until you secure the flash rate that seems the most hypnotic.

In using the device, request the spectators to relax back in their seats and to direct their gaze at the reflected light in the mirrors (See Fig. 107). Then start the turntable, and apply your mass hypnotic techniques. The rhythmic flashes of light produced by this machine are highly hypnotic.

The Rhythmic Light: Another effective "fixation object" for stage use you can make by rigging a light to the top of the "meter stick" of a metronome (See Fig. 108). Since the speed of this device can be varied you can easily set its rhythm to a hypnotic pace, and the ticking of the machine in time with the swinging light is decidedly sleep inducing. Used in semi-darkness, the eyes of your subjects following the Rhythmic Light, this machine will quickly produce hypnosis.

FIG. 107

FIG. 108

Electrical Hypnosis: A novelty method of hypnotizing that will add drama and variety in hypnotizing a subject on the stage is to make use of the familiar electrical device called, "The Jacob Ladder." This is made from a high tension transformer to the outputs of which are set two upright metal rods. Since these rods are spaced at an angle, when the spark arcs across it runs up the rods disappearing at their tops as it breaks. As the arc thus climbs up the rods, spark following spark, a ladder-like effect of bluish electric flame is produced (See Fig. 109).

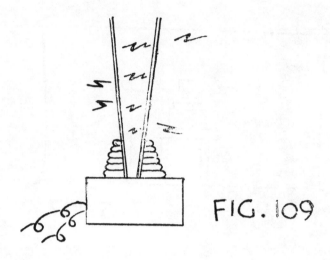

FIG. 109

In using this machine, seat the subject in front of it, advising him that you will hypnotize him by electrical means (here we have another example of hypnotic misdirection), and tell him to keep watching the sparks as they climb up the ladder. Then switch on the current and follow your formula for hypnotizing.

There is no especial hypnotic rhythm to the sparks so the value of this device comes purely from its attention arousing qualities. Performed in dim stage lights it is very spectacular. Use this machine on only one subject at a time, and only with subjects that have previously proven themselves susceptible to hypnotic influence. **A word of warning;** in using this device—keep your subjects away from it as there is some 50,000 volts of high tension current passing across the poles of the transformer.

The Audio Oscillator: Here is one of the most unsuspected secrets the Stage Hypnotist can apply. Have just behind your front wing an audio oscillator fitted with a "tweeter" type of speaker so as to produce a very high pitched sound (See Fig. 110). Regulate the sound frequency of the oscillator so the etxremely high note it produces is just out of the audible sound range of the human ear. Now for some reason yet to be determined, such a sound frequency tends to increase suggestibility. Consciously it cannot be heard, but unconsciously that continuous, inaudible sound makes it mark on the minds of your subjects and your audience, and renders them more susceptible to your hypnotic influence. Here is a device with laurels unseen and "unheard" that does a job for you throughout your entire hypnotic show.

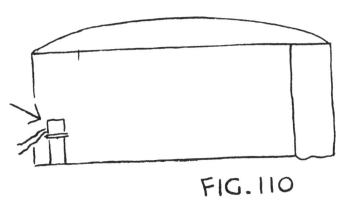

FIG. 110

AND IN CONCLUSION

With the scope of knowledge that now lies before you, is it any wonder that the success of the hypnotic show becomes 100 per cent a certainty, and that the marvels of Hypnotism that can be produced through the conditions of the stage leave audiences gasping and puzzle even trained psychologists and medical men well versed in Hypnotism. These are your secrets, and, precisely as in Magic, guard the tricks of your trade well. The science of Hypnotism you can discuss with all frankness, but the subtleties of Stage Hypnotism are **FOR MAGICIANS ONLY!**

The field of Stage Hypnotism is vast, and the scope and possibilities of developing the hypnotic show infinite. It can be staged as simply as the suit-case Magic Act, or as pretentiously as the gigantic illusion show, but whatever the status you select, **make all of your work an Art.**

You now have the knowledge of how to hypnotize, how to present, routine, and stage the hypnotic show; nothing remains but to apply with skill that knowledge. And such is your province as a magical showman.

As a last word of advice, I cannot do better than to recommend that you steep yourself in hypnotic literature. **Read everything you can get your hands on.** A visit to the library will reward you with many titles. Study the old classics of Moll, Bernheim, Binet and Féré, Forel, Bramwell, Sextus, Hudson, etc. And read such contemporary books as "Hypnotism" by Estabrooks, "What Is Hypnosis" by Salter, "Instantaneous

300

Hypnotism" by Nelmar, "Hypnotism" by De Laurence, "Practical Lessons In Hypnotism" by Wesley Cook, "Practical Hypnotism" by Ed Wolff, "Scientific Hypnotism" by Winn, "You Can Hypnotize Yourself and Others" by Victor Dane, "Hypnotism Today" by Le-Crown and Bordeaux, "Suggestion and Autosuggestion" by Charles Baudouin, etc.

In your study of Hypnotism you will notice many conflicts in theory, especially between the animal magnetism and the suggestion enthusiasts. But, to yor as a Magician, such makes little difference. It all ıorms knowledge, and with the assimilation of that knowledge **Hypnotism will become second nature to you.** Then, and then only, will you really be a Hypnotist. So talk it, read it, study it, and above all practice it. As Howard Thurston once advised, "If you want to be a successful Magician, three things are essential—practice, practice, and more practice"; such applies with equal force to Hypnotism.

And in closing, let me go on record as stating that your entire success as a Hypnotist will be summed up in t¹ one word—**Faith. Faith in yourself compelling the faith of your subjects and your audience is the law of the great Hypnotist.**

CPSIA information can be obtained
at www.ICGtesting.com
Printed in the USA
BVHW032327251119
564686BV00004B/36/P

9 781578 988716